How to go to sleep...

...and stay there

How to go to sleep...

...and stay there

Stephen Giles

Editor: Roni Jay

Viva Books

New Delhi | Mumbai | Chennai | Kolkata | Bangalore | Hyderabad | Kochi | Guwahati

First Indian Edition 2010

VIVA BOOKS PRIVATE LIMITED

- 4737/23 Ansari Road, Daryaganj, New Delhi 110 002
  E-mail: vivadelhi@vivagroupindia.net, Tel. 42242200
- 76, Service Industries, Shirvane, Sector 1, Nerul, Navi Mumbai 400 706
  E-mail: vivamumbai@vivagroupindia.net, Tel. 27721273, 27721274
- Jamals Fazal Chambers, 26 Greams Road, Chennai 600 006
  E-mail: vivachennai@vivagroupindia.net, Tel. 28290304, 28294241
- B-103, Jindal Towers, 21/1A/3 Darga Road, Kolkata 700 017
  E-mail: vivakolkata@vivagroupindia.net, Tel. 22836381, 22816713
- 7, Sovereign Park Apartments, 56-58, K. R. Road, Basavanagudi, Bangalore 560 004
  E-mail: vivabangalore@vivagroupindia.net, Tel. 26607409, 26607410
- 101-102 Mughal Marc Apartments, 3-4-637 to 641, Narayanguda, Hyderabad 500 029
  E-mail: vivahyderabad@vivagroupindia.net, Tel. 27564481, 27564482
- Beevi Towers, First Floor, SRM Road, Kaloor, Kochi 682 018, Kerala
  E-mail: vivakochi@vivagroupindia.net, Tel: 0484-2403055, 2403056
- 232, GNB Road, Beside UCO Bank, Silpukhuri, Guwahati 781 003
  E-mail: vivaguwahati@vivagroupindia.net, Tel: 0361-2666386

www.vivagroupindia.com

Published by arrangement with

Crimson Publishing,
a division of Crimson Business Ltd
Westminster House, Kew Road
Richmond, Surrey TW9 2ND

ISBN : 978-81-309-1484-8

Published by Vinod Vasishtha for Viva Books Private Limited, 4737/23, Ansari Road, Daryaganj, New Delhi - 110 002.

Printed and bound by Raj Press, R-3, Inderpuri, New Delhi - 110 012.

To David Burke – sleep well, my friend.

Acknowledgements

Sincere thanks are due to the following for their time, guidance and support during the writing of this book: Professor Kevin Morgan, Glenn Harrold, Sally Child, Andrew Kirk, Robert Gray, Josephine Hayward, Jessica Alexander, Roger Coghill, Zoe Archer, Claudia Roe, Samantha Lambert, Marianne Davey, Marian Casey, Lisa Sherman, Jon Smith, Leo Biddle, Lynn Wooding, Alan Hayman, Wendy Hayman, Sarah Davies, Daphne Giles, Barry Giles, Paul Giles, Jessica Ruston, Jack Ruston, Rosie Staal, Cormac Scanlan, Richard Hallows, Nikola Mann, Louise Peartree, Caroline Doughty, Colin Burden and all the surveyed sleepers. Particular thanks to Roni and the team at White Ladder, to Lindsay as ever, and to Oliver and George for sleeping at least some of the time.

Important note

None of the opinions offered or treatments discussed in this book are intended to replace medical opinion. If you have concerns regarding your own sleep problems, please seek professional treatment. Neither the author nor White Ladder Press can accept any responsibility for any injuries, damages or losses suffered as a result of following the information herein.

Contents

Introduction: Who needs sleep?

Answer: everyone. Sleep is as essential to the human condition as breathing. It keeps our brains functioning correctly and without it we'd literally go mad. And yet back in the 1980s, in those glory days of power suited yuppies with stiff jaws and floppy hair, some bold go-getter coined the phrase 'sleep is for wimps', a corruption of über yuppie Gordon Gekko's assertion in the film Wall Street that 'lunch is for wimps', and an explicit challenge to the previously held assumption that sleep, like lunch, was in fact a vital and mundane part of everyday life.

While the striped shirts and half-brick mobile phones of Maggie's children have now faded into the memory, this trite piece of posturing has somehow remained, its indelible mark spreading like an inky stain across the mass consciousness. Now it has a 'noughties' equivalent – 'you snooze, you lose' – which is equally explicit in its assumption that sleeping is an inherent sign of weakness.

Sleep, these maxims of machismo assure us, is a nuisance, an annoyance keeping us from the many and various opportunities presented by our online, instant access 24 hour existence. Sleep is viewed in some quarters with all the appeal of those roast beef pills that astronauts eat in science fiction films. Indeed one US pharmaceutical firm is pioneering just such a pill for people who want to stay awake all night every night, but who don't want the negative side effects. The consumer who never sleeps is the advertiser's ultimate dream and this poor dope will exist, and soon.

But for now there are enough people in the world who believe that a good night's sleep is an essential and highly beneficial aid to functioning as a normal part of society. The main difficulty lies in overcoming the obstacles that everyday life puts in the way. In this book we're going to take a look at the whole concept of sleep – analysing sleeplessness in general as well as some of the more serious problems that affect those of us who struggle to sleep, either on a regular basis or simply from time to time.

The flipside to the yuppie anti-sleep attitude is the growing band of 'lifestyle experts' whose job it is to persuade us all that we aren't sleeping enough, or that we're all sleeping much less than we used to – a claim that most serious sleep researchers deny. Their solutions inevitably come at a cost, but do they have any real benefit? Most people think that they need around eight hours sleep, but is this true, or simply a convenient sound bite cooked up by marketing men to peddle some more treatments?

To examine these questions fully, we'll start by looking at some of the preconceptions that people have about sleep and sleep patterns and will then go into greater detail about three key areas for better sleep – creating the right sleep environment, creating the right sleep routine and seeking help and guidance for more serious sleep disorders.

Along the way we'll tap into the stories of some willing 'guinea pigs' whose own sleep experiences have been recorded for this book, and who have agreed to try out some new treatments, therapies and theories for the sake of research. These 'guinea pigs' come from a range of backgrounds and have experienced sleeplessness with varying degrees of severity. We'll keep looking in on them as they hunt for the best way to manage their own quest to get to sleep or stay asleep.

Another key part of this book is the information provided by a team of willing helpers who have contributed to an in-depth survey of their sleep patterns and habits. As well as making reference to the results of this survey throughout the book, we will also pick out some of the nuggets of advice they pass on for other sleepers.

The most important thing to bear in mind when reading this book is that it's written without agenda. Within these pages, a variety of experts from all parts of the spectrum of conventional and alternative medicine and therapy put the case for their favoured theories in compelling and persuasive ways, but there's no definitive 'right' answer to such a subjective debate. There is evidence to be weighed up on all sides and then there is the effectiveness of any treatment or therapy in your specific case. Beyond this, no-one can tell you what should work for you and what shouldn't.

So read this book and when something strikes a chord follow it up, try it for yourself and see if it helps. This is not a book of easy answers, it's a book of signposts and suggestions for you to follow and examine so that you may find the right answers at your own pace. All the pieces of the jigsaw are here – it's up to you to find the right order and sequence for your individual needs.

Sleep is a precious part of life, and when it goes wrong it can colour everything else we do, think and feel – which is why less civilised societies use sleep deprivation as such an effective torture device. Sleep has such a powerful effect on our well-being that it demands our complete respect. This book aims to give sleep the respect it deserves, to reclaim it from the insatiable beasts of advertising and the workaholics who want to eliminate sleep's creative and restorative qualities.

By the time you've finished reading this book you'll have a clearer understanding of the structure, fragility and value of sleep, as well as some valuable and practical tips on how to ensure that you enjoy the best possible night's rest, every night.

Now, are you sitting comfortably? Then it's time for bed...

PART ONE:
How do you sleep?

It's easy to see why there's so much confusion surrounding the business of sleep. We're constantly bombarded with different theories on how much we need, what constitutes 'quality' sleep, whether napping is an effective way to catch up on sleep, and a bucketful of myths and half-truths that we're sometimes too ready to accept as fact. Part of the problem is that the various experts who advise on sleep use a startling range of definitions for the problems surrounding the subject. So before we begin our journey into sleep we need to define a few key terms and dispel some of the more common myths about sleeping. Let's start with the oldest chestnut on the tree:

Ok, the one thing I know about sleep is that everyone needs a good eight hours each night, right?

You couldn't be more wrong. This is a classically misleading statement of intent – usually wrapped up in the neat assertion that the work, rest and play periods of any given day should be divided into equal thirds. It's a tidy theory, but if life was really that simple we'd all be living in communes and driving Ladas. Just as the average junior doctor may well scoff bitterly at the concept of a gentle eight hour day, so the eight hour night is a purely subjective, and potentially damaging, goal.

According to Professor Kevin Morgan of the University of Loughborough's Sleep Research Centre, the amount of sleep we require is determined by a much deeper force than some desire to segment our lives along neat lines. He says: "Just as people have different appetites and different levels of stamina, there are different sleep needs built into their constitutions. You might find that you have a body that only needs five hours sleep a night, but that is not insomnia, that is simply having an inconvenient sleep schedule that nevertheless delivers you refreshed the next day. Similarly, some people find they need more than average sleep and they only feel rested after eight or nine hours."

This huge variety in sleep patterns is certainly represented in the sleep survey conducted for this book, with respondents' sleep duration varying in range from four hours a night to 10 hours a night. The average, taken across all responses, is in fact six hours 40 minutes a night – a long way short of the fabled eight hours. And yet, when asked, the respondents felt that their 'ideal' number of hours sleep would be an average of – yes, you guessed it – eight hours a night. But did the surveyed sleepers reach this figure because of conditioning, or because of a deep understanding of their own sleep pattern?

The British Association for Counselling and Psychotherapy conducted its own survey into sleep patterns and found that the national average sleep per night is incredibly close to our own survey's results at 6 hours and 53 minutes – a level, they claim, that suggests widespread sleep deprivation.

We need to know the best way to define how much sleep we need. The answer, according to Kevin Morgan, is intensely personal and purely operational: "You need as much sleep as is required to send you into the next day feeling alert and able to meet the demands of that day," he explains. "Beyond that there's nothing more to be said."

The fact that we're all individuals makes life more interesting, but it can also be a source of frustration, particularly if you're a nine hour long haul sleeper married to a five hour quick fix sleeper. As mentioned above, there's no point in trying to deny your sleep pattern, or to adjust it to suit someone else's. As we'll see later, your mental attitude towards the bed and bedroom forms a crucial part of a successful sleep pattern, so you could be doing yourself serious harm by lying awake for hours in bed just to spend more time with your slumbering partner.

Instead, as Kevin Morgan advises, you should trust and act upon your own in-built sleep instinct. "The individual knows best," he adds. "It's built into our psyche from the start of adulthood. People read themselves well and if we just attended to the results of that reading we wouldn't legislate so aggressively for what people should and shouldn't be doing with their sleep."

What do you mean by terms like 'good' and 'poor' sleep, surely all sleep is the same?

Not really. On an average night we go through a series of sleep stages, with both REM (Rapid Eye Movement) and non-REM sleep within recurring cycles of around two hours' duration. We begin in non-REM sleep, which is further subdivided into four sections, ranging from light sleep via true sleep to two levels of deep sleep. REM sleep is the stage that follows deep sleep.

REM sleep is the stage in which we are most likely to experience vivid dreams, as it is when the brain is at its most active – hence the flickering eyes – though our bodies are inert. It was previously believed that REM sleep was the only stage in which we dream, but we now know that dreams can occur all night.

On a bad or broken night we may never settle sufficiently to achieve the truly 'deep' sleep which our brains and bodies require to become revitalised through tissue replenishment and other essential preparations for the rigours of a new day. So a few concentrated hours of good, deep sleep is better for us than a long night of tossing and turning in poor sleep.

So how many people actually have sleep problems?

This is quite difficult to quantify exactly, because many people will suffer from poor sleep on a regular basis but they won't necessarily do anything about it – either by convincing themselves that there's nothing untoward about their sleep pattern, or because of the slightly more cynical belief that there's not much they can do to make things better. The best estimates show that around one fifth of all adults in the UK suffer from sleep problems at night that cause serious sleepiness in the day.

The British Association for Counselling and Psychotherapy survey breaks these statistics down still further, suggesting that more than a quarter of the UK's adult population (12 million people) experience at least three bad night's sleep in an average week. Seven million people find that the majority of nights are bad and three million suffer a bad night's sleep every night.

But there's nothing actually wrong with being a bit short of sleep, is there?

That rather depends on your definition of 'a bit'. Thousands of accidents are linked directly to tiredness each year. In 2004 a group of medics, sleep disorder experts, accident prevention experts and other interested parties banded together as the Sleep Alliance to produce the Sleep SOS Report. This report called for a more proactive approach to sleep disorders and excessive tiredness in society, and quoted some pretty stark statistics for anyone who thinks it's acceptable to be sleepy most of the time.

For example, more fatal accidents are caused by sleepiness each year than by drink-driving – and not just at night but also during the afternoon 'dip' in wakefulness. And that's just the risk to drivers, passengers and pedestrians – sleepiness can also lead to dangerous lapses of judgment in the home or at work, especially for those people operating machinery.

> **More than 300 people die on the roads each year as a direct result of sleepiness.**

Add to this potential horror show the very real possibility that excessive sleepiness undermines relationships with friends, family and colleagues and you start to build a picture of a condition that is akin to alcoholism or drug abuse in its antisocial impact. And yet most people still regard chronic sleeplessness as a normal part of an average busy day.

Of course, the root cause of this misery may not be simply that you aren't sleeping enough, there's a whole host of sleep disorders that can impact on the quality and restorative value of sleep (see below and parts four and five). But either way the essential message is that doing nothing is not an option. Your mental health, your relationships and even people's lives are at stake if excessive sleepiness goes unchecked.

What does the term circadian rhythm mean? It sounds like something out of a sci-fi movie.

It certainly does. But it's actually very down to earth. You might commonly refer to it as your 'body clock' – the innate system which tells us when it's time for sleep (preferably in the dark and at night) and when it's time to be awake (daylight, birds singing, children playing etc.). When your circadian rhythm is disturbed or becomes faulty – for example during changing shift work patterns or as a consequence of jet lag, your sleep pattern can be seriously affected. We'll talk more about this in part five.

What are serotonin and melatonin, and what part do they play in helping us sleep?

Good question, you're really getting into this now. Ok, the brief and simplistic answer is as follows – serotonin is a substance produced in the pineal gland in the human brain. It is known in pharmacology as 5-HT. It acts as a neurotransmitter, helping to balance our mood, our sleep pattern, even our temperature, and low levels of serotonin may be linked to depression and other illnesses. It is an incredibly versatile and powerful substance, especially given the relatively small amounts of serotonin present in the average person. Various foods and food supplements are thought to stimulate the production of serotonin. You can find out more about these in part three.

The pineal gland also produces melatonin. This hormone is only produced when the environment is dark and therefore helps maintain the circadian rhythm by making us sleepy at the right time. Melatonin production peaks in the middle of the night and then gradually falls away. It is widely believed that melatonin production also drops away as we age. There is a large industry (mainly in the US) that advocates the use of melatonin as a supplement for people – particularly the elderly – who have a problem sleeping or who may have difficulty producing sufficiently high levels of melatonin. These supplements are not licensed in the UK, and they are not widely supported among conventional or alternative healthcare professionals. The power of melatonin and the UK scientist who is using melatonin in a revolutionary way are discussed in more detail in part three.

Old people are always dropping off to sleep, so as you get older, you must sleep more, right?

I can see where you're coming from. Plenty of us have childhood memories of waiting impatiently for our grandparents to get up on Christmas morning, or of sitting amazed as an elderly relative manages to snore all the way through an afternoon movie. So it's fairly logical to assume that old folks spend more time asleep.

But that's simply not the case, as Kevin Morgan explains: "As we get older we don't sleep so much or at the same time at night. Our sleep will become shorter, lighter and more fragmented."

One in three people over 70 have a chronic sleep problem and around half of these actively seek treatment for their shortage of sleep. That's quite a sizeable chunk of an ever growing segment of our society. But Kevin Morgan takes the alternative view that although all older people sleep less well, two thirds of them just get on with life, bearing out his theory that the individual remains the best judge of whether the sleep they are getting is sufficient for their daily needs.

So should we follow their example and give in to an afternoon nap?

If you are a bit short of sleep and you're lucky enough to be able to manage a short nap – and not get fired while doing so – it's not necessarily a bad thing. There's quite a lot of evidence to suggest that a quick afternoon nap is part of our essential make-up as humans – after all it's a habit we form as babies and toddlers and only really drop because of the demands of a full day. Many adults still feel a drop in wakefulness in the post-lunch period, which may also explain why siestas are still popular in hot countries, using the logical theory that if you can't do anything useful in the heat, you might as well catch up on your sleep. In France, there have even been moves to enshrine the right to a daily nap into employment law.

People with more relaxed routines, such as the retired (and writers) often find a short afternoon nap is as effective as a few extra hours in bed at night, and if you find yourself excessively tired in the day it goes without saying that a short nap is better for you than trying to function while exhausted.

You mention the word routine – how important is this for a good sleep pattern?

Routine is vital for sleep and if you can sustain a pattern of going to bed and getting up at regular times, you're more likely to sleep well. The same advice holds true for those occasional bad nights due to a late party, being woken by your children, or some external factor (like singing cats or fireworks going off outside your window). You're much better off trying to keep your usual routine intact, even if you feel a bit chewed up the next day – if you lie in or try to sleep earlier than usual the following night, you'll find sleep harder to come by and this may ultimately lead to more problems.

Try telling that to my teenagers – they're always late to bed and they won't get up in the morning.

Yes, well as usual teenagers are a bit of an exception. During the teenage years, the circadian rhythm switches over from the 10 or 12 hour nights of a child into a shorter, adult pattern. Unfortunately, few teenagers fancy the idea of graduating this switch by getting early nights until the change has bedded in – meaning they are often short of sleep. The circadian rhythm disorder known as delayed sleep phase syndrome (DSPS) is particularly common in teenagers (see part five for more details). The circadian rhythm is usually something that can be readjusted through a combination of lifestyle changes and, in more chronic cases, drugs or therapy.

I do get insomnia, but it's only mild and occasional, so I just put up with it.

Be careful now. The term insomnia is used frequently, and not always wisely, to describe poor sleep in general. Some health professionals talk of mild (or transient) insomnia, short term insomnia and long term (or chronic) insomnia. This clearly suggests that insomnia has degrees of severity, and that treatment can be varied according to the symptoms shown by the sufferer.

Other sleep researchers and academics, including Kevin Morgan and his colleagues at the Sleep Research Centre in

Loughborough, follow a more rigid definition, as set down by the rather daunting Diagnostic and Statistical Manual of the American Psychiatric Association – fourth edition, which is thankfully known as DSM-IV for short. This manual classifies insomnia as a complaint of getting to sleep, or staying asleep or a complaint of non-restorative sleep that disturbs the individual at least three times a week and has occurred for at least the previous month. The symptoms must be of sufficient severity to have an impact on social and occupational functioning during the day.

And that's it, in a rather large nutshell. In clinical terms, which are the terms we'll be using in this book, that is insomnia. Of course, as Kevin Morgan adds, it is possible to talk about any episode of sleeplessness as insomnia, but you won't necessarily get the right treatment. He explains: "If you want to colloquialise both the notion of insomnia and approaches to management, then you can define it as you please. You can call it what you want – provided you know why you're calling it what you're calling it."

In short, don't confuse your terms if you want effective treatment. Insomnia is always a chronic state and it can, and should, be categorised in very specific terms.

Why have you called this book How to go to sleep – and stay there? What's the difference?

Another good question, with another complicated answer. Let's talk specifically about insomnia, first of all – this is correctly categorised using the terms outlined in the answer above, though it does exist in two 'states' – as sleep onset insomnia (how to get to sleep) and sleep maintenance insomnia (how to stay there).

Because there are two states of insomnia, there are different ways to approach each problem. Treatments, such as those discussed in part four, will take the relevant state of insomnia into account. In our discussions of general sleeplessness, it's worth our while making the same split – as most of the sleep hygiene recommendations in parts two and three relate to sleep onset (which is the most common form of sleeplessness) but some can specifically be used to help get the sleeper back to sleep in the middle of the night.

So if you can't sleep or you feel tired all the time, you've got insomnia, right?

Just as it is important that we know what insomnia is, it's also vital to know what it isn't, or rather that insomnia is not some catch-all expression for sleeping disorders.

In total there are a mind numbing 88 different categories of recognised and proposed sleep disorders as laid out in the International Classification of Sleep Disorders. Some of these disorders are associated with other medical conditions, like epilepsy, asthma and dementia.

The main sub-categories of sleep disorder are parasomnias, including sleepwalking, night terrors and restless leg syndrome – in which an event happens to disturb the normal balance of sleep – and dyssomnias: disorders of the amount or quality of sleep including conditions such as obstructive sleep apnoea, narcolepsy and more 'transient' disorders like jet lag.

In part five we'll take a closer look at some of the more common disorders, and the range of treatment options currently available to sufferers.

Is there a particular personality type that's likely to be affected by insomnia or sleep disorders?

You might be on to something there. Kevin Morgan's research into sleep and ageing suggests that some people are more personally affected than others. He adds: "This points to an inherent constitutional vulnerability to sleep disturbances. Some people have a more fragile sleep and they have a mindset that copes less well with sleep disturbances. Sitting inside about a third of us, at all ages, is a person with insomnia, you just have to wait for the right circumstances. That might be age or other circumstances like childbirth."

It may also be linked to your gender, according to statistics thrown up by the British Association for Counselling and Psychotherapy's survey of sleep patterns. While 42 per cent of male respondents report no bad nights sleep, only 32 per cent of women did the same. In fact almost one in 10 women report a bad night's sleep every night. The reasons for this aren't clear, but it might simply be that men worry less than women. The male respondents were more likely to blame their sleep disturbances on external factors like alcohol, late night TV or computer usage and digestive problems, while women were more inclined to blame anxiety about work and family.

In the survey commissioned for this book, almost half of the women interviewed cited worries about home/relationships and work as key factors in sleep disturbance compared to just a quarter of men.

The comment earlier regarding childbirth leads us to another circumstance that is gender specific, namely the increased likelihood of sleep problems during pregnancy – sorry lads, but we don't count 'sleeping next to a gigantic, hot, angry woman' as a sleep disorder. For pregnant women, however, there's a good chance of experiencing at least one disorder over the course of the nine months of pregnancy – be it snoring, restless leg syndrome, or in cases of extreme stress in pregnancy, even chronic insomnia. Most of the advice contained in this book is safe for pregnant women to follow, but in specific cases – like the use of aromatherapy and some other alternative therapies – it is always wise to check the suitability of the treatment with a qualified practitioner first.

What about these 'guinea pigs' of yours? Who are they and what are their stories?

They're a collection of ordinary people with varying degrees of difficulty getting to sleep or staying asleep. I'm not going to tell you their real names because they've opened up a very private world for the sake of this book, but I will give you a potted history of each of them:

Annabel is in her early twenties. She's a student and she has chronic sleep problems. On average she manages around two to four hours each night, though her 'night' doesn't often begin until the dawn chorus. Her problems began during her teenage years and have steadily worsened. Now she fears that she'll never be able to get back into a normal sleep pattern – in fact the idea of a good night's sleep is so alien and daunting, she's even begun to resist it.

Barbara is at the other end of the scale. In her mid-sixties, she sleeps reasonably well, but wakes frequently in the night. She's been a light sleeper since having children and now finds her sleep is more easily interrupted than ever. She's looking for a remedy that will allow her to relax fully into sleep and go through the night without waking periods.

Carole is in her early thirties. She has recently started her own business and, with two small children, she finds it hard to switch off at night. She is often exhausted by the end of the day and is keen to find a solution that allows her to escape from her busy daily routine and relax into sleep.

Dean is in his mid-thirties. He's normally a heavy sleeper, who is used to an average of around eight hours a night. Since becoming a parent and working for himself, his sleep pattern has fragmented and he finds himself awake for long periods at night, worrying about work and family issues. He is looking for a way to relax himself back into sleep if he wakes during the night.

Emily is in her late thirties. She has a history of poor sleep that can be traced back over a variety of significant events in life. Her partner was a shift worker, she had a very tough pregnancy and more recently she suffered a bereavement. All of these episodes have left a major impression on Emily's sleep pattern. She finds it incredibly stressful to go to bed and sleeps only fitfully when she does eventually turn in. She is prepared to try whatever it takes to correct the balance of her sleep, as she fears it is intruding on her family life and her general well-being.

Frances is in her twenties. Her sleep pattern has fluctuated between fair and poor over the last decade, during which time she's lived in some fairly noisy environments in a busy city. She's keen to regulate her sleep pattern and ensure that outside disturbance doesn't intrude too much on her nights.

Gloria is in her mid-fifties. She's experienced a variety of sleep problems at various stages of life – including serious problems as a new mother, during the menopause and while caring for an elderly relative. Frustrated by conventional medicine, Gloria is determined to sample alternative treatments for her sleep problems.

Finally, what is sleep hygiene, and does it have anything to do with showering before bed?

Good guess, but no. Good sleep hygiene is concerned with creating the best possible sleeping environment and personal pre-sleep routine. If you want to improve the efficiency and effectiveness of your sleep, there's a huge range of things you can try. These vary from the bizarre to the mundane, from the expensive to the free of charge. They're also likely to vary in effectiveness from sleeper to sleeper.

Over the course of parts two and three, we're going to look in greater depth at some of the more widespread methods that claim to improve sleep. Again, it's important to stress that these are not cures for insomnia or for any sleep disorders; they are simply strategies for positively altering the place where you sleep and your state of mind prior to sleeping.

KEY POINTS:

Don't obsess about getting your eight hours – there's no 'ideal' length of sleep. You need enough sleep to send you into the next day functioning fully, which may mean 10 hours, or it may mean five. Trust your instincts.

Keep to a routine. Get up and go to bed at roughly the

same times each day – even if you've had a bad night. Routine encourages a good sleep pattern, so cut out the early nights and the lying-in.

As we age we sleep less – but that doesn't mean we need less sleep. Older people experience more sleep problems than younger people, it's an inevitable part of the ageing process.

Know your terms. A bad night's sleep is just that – it's not insomnia. Insomnia is a chronic condition established over a period which has a major impact on your daily life.

Sleep problems may be caused by a range of factors. Poor sleep environment and an insufficiently relaxing pre-sleep routine are possible contributors. But you may also be suffering from a sleep disorder, which will require specific treatment or management.

PART TWO: In my room – the sleep environment

Q: How do you get a good night's sleep?

A: I love the pleasurable feeling of climbing into a bed made with freshly laundered sheets – linen preferably, but good cotton will do. It's comforting and therefore sleep-inducing.

In this section we'll be considering a wide range of factors that may influence the quality and effectiveness of the sleeping environment. For pretty much everyone, this means the bedroom – though one survey respondent does admit to sleeping in the garden on a regular basis. We don't tend to give too much thought to the bedroom, or to the outside influences that may be affecting the quality of our sleep, but over the course of this section we'll start to put together a practical list of essentials for the ultimate restful room.

We'll be looking at the following environmental factors:

★ light and noise pollution

★ the impact of electromagnetic fields and microwaves

★ geopathic stress

★ beds and mattresses

★ temperature in the bedroom

★ room design – clutter, artwork and colour

★ room lighting

★ bed position

★ home security

Lights, camera, action, sleep.

I don't want to worry you, but you may be under attack. Just when you thought it was safe to go back into the bedroom, a plethora of potential pollutants awaits the sleeper. We're not talking about the kind of pollution that follows a spicy curry the night before, although that's not particularly conducive to a positive sleep environment, either. No, the types of pollution we're going to be looking at here come from a range of sources – namely noise, light, electromagnetic fields (EMFs) and microwaves.

Let's start with noise. It's a troublesome issue and, in common with many sleep related topics, it's a very political one. Traffic noise, aircraft noise and noise entering poorly soundproofed houses – either from neighbouring properties or from outside – are all major factors affecting sleepers.

Campaigning website noiseresource.org reports that traffic noise accounts for two-thirds of all the noise generated outside UK homes. This traffic noise averages between 55 and 75 decibels, which the World Health Organisation regards as an intrusive level. The impact of aircraft noise isn't so widespread, but it's still felt by the 600,000 people living in the vicinity of the country's major airports, who experience noise pollution around 54-55 decibels. Adequate soundproofing is not currently a standard requirement for UK social housing, and many private homes are built to a low standard, with residents complaining of the intrusive sound of neighbours just going about their daily business.

According to research conducted by the Dutch Department of Environmental Health, people who suffer sleep disturbance due to outside noise are most likely to be aware of aircraft noise, then traffic noise and then finally railway noise, even if all three noises are at the same level. The same study found that the age at which noise disturbance is most likely to cause a reaction to the sleeper is between 50 and 56 years.

The sure fire solution to all this racket is to cut flights, slow traffic and build better houses. But back in the real world, the solution is usually much closer to home. Your first option is to block unwelcome noise using a sound shield like earplugs. These might seem a bit cumbersome, but they've become a big business and now come in a wide range of styles and materials.

Internet shops like snorestore.co.uk stock silicone and foam earplugs for adults and children in a dazzling variety of styles and comfort options. There are even earplugs which only block certain types of noise.

Of course, earplugs will only work if you're comfortable wearing them, and if you're relaxed with the idea that you'll hear nothing else around you, which probably rules out just about anyone who's the parent of a young child.

Beyond simply blocking out the intrusion of noise, there are other obvious barriers against outside noise – like installing double glazing or doing what the house builder failed to and sticking an extra layer of plasterboard on a party wall. Even re-arranging your furniture as a sound block or sticking some (filled) bookshelves on the party wall could help lessen the impact of intrusive noise caused by inadequate insulation.

Even if your house has adequate soundproofing, there are some neighbours who just demand to be heard, as the miserable blight of noisy neighbours is an ever growing issue. Some local authorities have even established teams to monitor and combat the effect of noise disturbance. Your local council is the best place to begin if you have a complaint or a query about neighbourhood noise. Their environmental health team or dedicated noise patrol will be able to measure the level of noise pollution and take appropriate action against the offenders. Don't expect these noise crusaders to be able to work miracles against the people down the road who have a one-off, impromptu party – their real goal is to crack down on persistent and regular din-makers like pubs, nightclubs and those pesky kids in the bus shelter.

Tackling persistent noise is not an easy job, and though the associated lack of sleep may be driving you to distraction, please resist the temptation to challenge your noisy neighbours. If people can get themselves sent to prison over a few fast growing leylandii, just imagine what damage you could do, or have done to you, by shouting the odds over someone's full volume Barry Manilow. Leave it to the authorities.

Overall, the impact of noise pollution is hard to quantify. Whenever you move house there's new noises to deal with, and most people feel that they will eventually adjust to a noisy sleeping environment as they become more familiar with the sounds around them. But noiseresource.org reports that this thinking can lead to a misconception about quality of sleep in a noisy environment, as noise can cause increased heart rate and blood pressure levels, leading to poorer, shallower sleep.

Light pollution is an equally intrusive nuisance, though happily it is usually a lot easier to tackle. The intense glow of a street light can be a real pain, which is why it's always good to view any house you're planning to buy after dark to check the intensity of any lights. If you live in an area without street lighting and the council installs it, there should be some consultation with residents over the positioning of the lights, though as this regularly leads to months of debate and recrimination, some councils may prefer to stick the lights in and wait for the flak.

The easiest and most effective way to lessen light pollution is to fit thicker curtains, though even these may not be completely effective in mitigating the glare of a street light. An eye mask is another alternative, which once more comes down to the question of comfort. Thick blackout blinds, such as those some people use in a baby's nursery, do work to good effect against the intrusion of natural light as the summer months draw in – they're also good for shift workers who want to create an artificially darkened environment for daytime sleeping.

Thick curtains aren't always a good solution in the bedroom, particularly for people who are less sensitive to light, as they may lead to a tendency to oversleep.

SLEEP DIARIES – NOISE AND LIGHT

FRANCES: *"I used both ear plugs and eye masks for approximately two years, mainly because the flat I was living in was unfortunately right on a main road and there was strong street lighting that would blaze in through the windows at night – not an ideal flat to live in if you have trouble sleeping! They did help though, but I found them generally to be a bit uncomfortable, especially when one of the ear plugs would dislodge."*

EMILY: *"My last house was on a main road and the street lighting was very intense. I used blackout blinds. I was alone and the neighbours were really noisy, there would often be rows in the middle of the night, screams and shouts. It was very frightening and disturbing. I could have complained, but they'd have known it was me and he really scared me. So in the end I moved. I didn't really have much choice, I never felt comfortable and my sleep was terrible."*

Electromagnetic fields (EMFs) and microwaves present a very different challenge to noise and light pollution. They are harder to define and measure, and the amount of research into their detrimental effects is more limited.

Once again, the research that has been carried out into this subject is highly politicised – as there's little government data available, the stage is open to pressure groups like **powerwatch.org.uk** which present stark and bleak claims about the insidious impact of microwaves and EMFs.

Outside of the house, the impact of established energy sources like pylons is low, but research into the impact of the many thousands of microwave antennae for mobile phones suggests a powerful but as yet unproven link with cancer and other adverse heatlh effects, including sleep disturbance.

The cynical view is that these antennae make millions of pounds of income for the state, so their damaging impact will never be effectively assessed or revealed, but the truth is that, whether there's a cover-up or just not enough quality research, we simply don't yet know enough about the impact of microwaves on our health. That shouldn't stop you being vigilant, and it should be enough to make you pressure your local MP into calling for the government to commission a truly independent assessment of the health risks associated with microwave antennae.

Inside the home, microwaves and EMFs are everywhere, thanks in part to the wonders of modern technology. Anyone with a wireless network or cordless phone will have a multitude of microwaves zinging their way around the place. Similarly, any live electrical appliances in the bedroom emit an EMF, for example, clock radio, lamp, mobile phone charger, a TV or laptop on standby. There's also EMF coming from any mains wiring running through the walls.

So it's clear that these invisible blighters are everywhere. The hard part is making the link between them and sleep disturbance. A number of studies, including some reported by powerwatch.org.uk, have produced interesting results, suggesting that EMFs can disrupt brain activity during sleep. Rather like noise pollution, this disruption may not be sufficient for the sleeper to be actively aware of the problem, but it may lead to poor sleep quality and efficiency and a reduction in the overall time asleep.

So if you're sufficiently convinced by the studies to take action against EMFs and microwaves, what options are open to you, beyond taking an axe to the nearest antennae (not recommended)? The answer might come from a slightly surprising area, given the modernity of the problem – the ancient art of Feng Shui.

Robert Gray, the founder of the Feng Shui Academy, and a member of the Feng Shui Society, tours the world giving seminars and advice on the practical application of Feng Shui principles to the modern world. He says: "The official Feng Shui Society definition says that Feng Shui is the practice of analysing and influencing the interaction between people, buildings and the environment in order to enhance the quality of life. It evolved out of the realisation that we are substantially affected by our environments."

But where do harmful microwaves fit in, after all isn't Feng Shui just about creating a calming and relaxing environment? That depends on your definition of the art, but as Robert Gray adds, there's precedent for all kinds of applications: "Even in ancient Feng Shui the principle of protection existed – situating a home to remain protected from harsh winds, or flooding. In modern society we need to be aware of invisible hazards, such as EMFs, and to know how to protect ourselves from them."

According to Robert, there are two essential methods of protecting your sleeping environment from the intrusion of EMFs and microwaves, these are avoidance and shielding.

He explains: "Locate electrical appliances a safe distance away from your sleeping area. This distance depends on the individual appliance, for instance some bedside lamps give off low fields, and these are fine positioned at an arm's stretch from the pillow. However, a mains powered clock radio will be safe if it is on the other side of the bedroom from the bed. It also becomes a better alarm clock, as you have to get out of bed to switch it off."

Avoiding mains wiring is a bit more of a trial and error scenario, as the level of EMF given off by the wiring varies enormously from house to house. He adds: "Sometimes pulling the bed away from the wall by 15cm is enough, sometimes two metres is not enough, but in all cases, the further away you are from the source, the lower the intensity of the field."

To lessen the likelihood of interference from microwaves in the bedroom, switch back to a traditional wired telephone and wired internet connection or home network rather than the wireless alternatives.

In terms of shielding, there are two fairly new options available. Robert explains: "A special shielding paint can be applied on a wall or under the carpet, if microwaves are coming from below as might be the case in a block of flats or from a wireless network downstairs in a two storey home. The other option is a nickel based shielding fabric which can be used like a net curtain on a window or around a bed. I have what looks like a mosquito net around my bed, but actually it is the shielding fabric to protect me from the microwaves from nearby mobile phone antennae."

SLEEP DIARY – EMF AND MICROWAVES

DEAN: *"I've always felt instinctively that things like mobile phone chargers shouldn't be in the bedroom, but that's more to do with the irritating low hum they give off. I can't stand any background noise in the bedroom, and that's why I use a clock radio instead of an old-fashioned alarm clock. But I wanted to try and cut interference from EMFs, so I moved the bed onto an outside wall with no power cables and I put the clock on the other side of the room. It's hard to say whether it's made much difference to my sleep over the couple of weeks since I made the changes. I gave up on the alarm clock idea pretty quickly, as I like to be able to see it easily in the night. Instead I just bought a battery powered clock. But moving the bed does seem to have helped. Only trouble is, I'm a bit worried about outside noise now."*

If it's not enough that we're under attack from EMFs and microwaves, the planet may well be conspiring to disrupt our sleep as well. At least that's the theory behind another concept used widely in Feng Shui – the identification and management of geopathic stress.

According to Robert Gray, geopathic stress can be defined as a distortion of the Earth's natural energy field (which normally resonates around 7.83hz) causing harmful radiation to emanate from the Earth's surface. If you happen to have your home situated on one or more geopathic stress lines, there can also be significant consequences for your well-being – including poor sleep, frequent illness and even depression.

Apparently it can be caused by both natural and human factors, including subterranean running water, certain mineral formations, underground fault lines and cavities. When we dig up the earth or explode it when quarrying or mining, we can disrupt these natural low vibrations for miles around and this causes geopathic stress.

Detecting geopathic stress is, fortunately, a fairly straightforward process, using the art of dowsing. Dowsers use their bodies, dowsing rods or a pendulum to identify the source of the stress. You can engage the services of a dowser, or better still you can learn the art yourself. Robert Gray's Feng Shui Academy runs courses on dowsing, and while live tuition is most effective, it's also possible to learn the art from a range of books on the subject.

But before you rush off to retrain as a dowser, how can you be sure that geopathic stress lies at the heart of your sleep problems? It's a matter of making links between your house and your health, as Robert Gray explains: "You have to think, did my problem coincide with or begin shortly after moving into this home? Do I feel better, sometimes immediately, upon leaving the place? How well do you sleep when away from the home altogether? Has anyone commented on any feelings of uneasiness here? You could ask your friends or relatives. Can you find out if the previous occupants had any problem sleeping or suffered illness? Do you know of any work going on in the neighbourhood such as building or other earth disruption?"

So why does geopathic stress have such a profound and specific impact on sleep? Robert Gray explains: "Science tells us that at night when we sleep a lot of repairing and rebuilding is taking place in our bodies. It seems that when someone is sleeping in geopathic stress their resources are having to battle harder to deal with the harmful frequencies and so an illness can last longer or sleep can be restless or unpleasantly heavy."

So if you're concerned that geopathic stress may be at the root of your sleep and health problems, what steps can you take to tackle the underlying problem? Your first option is to employ an expert in geopathic stress detection and treatment to conduct a full survey of your home. Alternatively, take a course of study in order to do these things for yourself. If you'd rather not spend out at all, but you want to see if the theory works for you, simply try sleeping in a different place in the room or in another room altogether. Of course, a geopathic stress line may run through both positions.

If you discover a geopathic stress line in your bedroom, either through your own investigations or through a survey, the cures are many and various and can include the use of certain mineral crystals, symbols, and talismans placed strategically along the line. Robert Gray explains more: "Wherever possible I treat geopathic stress with 'Earth Acupuncture' which involves using wood, metal or stone to insert into a specific point along the line (usually in the garden or surrounding area). Combining this work with qigong [see part three] energy techniques makes for a very effective, long lasting and sometimes even permanent treatment. The usual result is that the line is harmonised and not diverted, bringing beneficial rather than harmful energy into the home. On no account should this be attempted without proper training or you could make the situation worse.

"Standing stones and stone cairns are another traditional cure, and fairly recently electronic devices have been invented which use the mains electrical circuit of your home to provide a sort of shield around it. I have found that these, at best, partially improve the situation."

And so to bed

Q: How do you get a good night's sleep?

A: Sleep alone.

Protecting your sleeping area is just half the battle. Your next major challenge comes in a variety of shapes, sizes, heights and comfort levels, and yet it's almost certain to be the one item in your house that you purchase without thought or consideration – your bed.

It stands to reason that an uncomfortable bed makes for a poor night's sleep, and yet according to the Sleep Council, an information service supported by bed manufacturers, a whopping 80 per cent of people spend less than two minutes choosing their bed. To put this in quantifiable terms, most of us spend less time selecting the furniture we'll use for around seven hours in each day than we spend talking to nuisance sales callers. How dumb is that?

Not as dumb as it may appear. The odds are stacked against the informed bed buyer by two fairly significant constraints. The first one hits us straight in the showroom. The people selling beds are rarely equipped with the knowledge of their products to provide a detailed assessment of individual needs.

The information is there, from the manufacturers, or from the Sleep Council, but the problem lies in persuading people to take their bed buying seriously. The Sleep Council's Jessica Alexander explains: "Buyers need to be more aware and informed – too many people are buying online or via mail order. We're trying to de-commoditise beds, to get people to try before they buy, but it's hard as you can't take a bed home on a trial basis – certainly most mattresses are non-refundable. While some manufacturers will exchange a bed in the first 40 days after purchase, the onus is on the buyer to spend more time in store and put more thought into their purchase."

The average length of time since our surveyed sleepers last changed their mattresses is three and a half years. There is no 'right' length of time to keep a mattress – if a sprung mattress is turned regularly and is a quality product it should stand a decade of constant use. But if your mattress has stopped providing the support you need, it's time for a change, even if it's a fairly recent purchase.

So to get us started, how do we go about deciding on the right bed for our individual needs? Jessica Alexander explains: "There are three key factors when choosing a bed, and particularly a mattress – comfort, support and size. Comfort is subjective, support is more easily measured, as it is determined by a correlation between weight and build, though there's no standard 'firmness' measurement chart, so again it is partly subjective. As a starting point you'd need a firmer mattress to support more weight – thus supporting the spine. An ideal mattress will provide cushioning to avoid pressure points. Many people like memory foam as it is good at pressure relieving support – this material started life in hospitals, where it was used for long term care patients."

A pain in the back

Of course bad mattresses can be bad for backs, as can bad pillows, and both should be chosen with care. Osteopaths treat their fair share of back complaints that are either caused by bad mattresses or that are significantly worsened by the lack of support from a bad mattress, so the General Osteopathic Council has developed its own tips for bed and mattress buying. These include the following points:

Turning. The majority of sprung mattresses will need to be turned frequently (ideally around every six weeks to three months). Foam and latex mattresses do not need turning.

Support. A good mattress is one that takes the weight of the body without sagging. Don't make a sudden change from a very soft bed to a very hard one, but do make sure your mattress is firm enough to allow for shifts of posture during the night.

Allergies. Allergic disorders such as asthma and eczema could be aggravated by sleeping on beds which harbour dust and mites. Hygiene and ventilation of the bed and covers are important – special protective covers may also help to keep dust at bay.

Sweat. The body loses between one and two pints of evaporated perspiration each night. If you use a board under your mattress to improve firmness, ensure that it has holes to allow for effective ventilation, otherwise perspiration build-up will rot the mattress.

Base. A high quality, heavy mattress will need a decent quality base if it is to be fully effective. Where possible you should try to buy the base and mattress together to ensure that the base is strong enough.

Shop testing. You should spend at least 20 minutes on a mattress in the shop to get a reasonable idea of its comfort level. That might seem a long time, but it's a lot shorter than the time you'll spend on it each night.

Water. Consider a water bed – these aren't suitable for everyone, but they are comfortable as they have no pressure points, they support the body without distorting the spine and will last for many years without sagging. As with all beds, these are a very subjective choice – try one before you buy.

Weight differences. If you and your partner differ significantly in size and weight, consider a 'zip and lock' bed which gives you the opportunity to have different mattress types on each side.

As far as the humble pillow is concerned, quality is far better than quantity. Too many pillows on the bed – or soft toys for that matter – can create back problems because of an awkward sleeping posture. Sleeping without a pillow puts the neck under similar strain. An orthopaedic pillow, or one that is made from memory foam, may be good alternatives for people who are prone to neck or back problems. And remember if you're sleeping away from home for any period – on a holiday, for example – take your pillow with you.

Size matters

So what's the official view on size, Jessica Alexander's third key criterion for bed buyers? She explains: "There's plenty of evidence available to suggest that size is an important issue, and that people's attitudes are changing. Over the last decade or so, larger sized beds have claimed between 20 and 30 per cent of the buying market."

The issue of size presents the second immovable object for the bed buyer – the shape and size of the modern bedroom. As homebuyers' expectations change, and space for new houses remains at a premium, many new homes are built with two bathrooms upstairs, one an en suite for the main bedroom. The desire to cram a study into the upstairs living space often means that a house that would previously have contained two fair sized bedrooms now contains three small rooms.

Jessica has watched this trend with interest. She says: "It's what I call the 'estate agents' double room syndrome'. A bedroom in a modern house might be big enough for a king size bed, but nothing else. People want wardrobes or chests of drawers. So they end up going for a standard double even if their size suggests they should buy a bigger bed."

Back to the rather stark response provided in one survey and reproduced above – is there any benefit to sleeping alone rather than sharing a bed? Jessica adds: "Yes, some research has been done to suggest that people, mainly women, do sleep better on their own than with a partner. This is more often the case as people get older." Could it be that twin beds are the answer you're looking for?

SLEEP DIARIES – BEDS AND MATTRESSES

ANNABEL: "The type of bed has always played a major part in my sleep. When I was at school my mum and dad bought me a new single bed that was really high. I had one night awake in it then slept on the floor until they changed it. So I learned that I sleep better in lower beds. Don't know why. Later I got a double bed (low, of course) and I actually think this helped at first. In my single bed I had got used to lying in certain positions, but I never slept. I found that in my double bed I was less organised in the way I slept and therefore got to sleep quicker and generally slept without waking up as much."

DEAN: "I spent a lot of money on a new, memory foam mattress a little while ago and it didn't seem to be helping at all. But then a few weeks back my bed frame actually broke (no, it's not what you think!) and I had to buy a new one. I probably didn't spend too long thinking about the choice, but I ended up buying one much higher than the old one. You actually have to climb into it, whereas the other one was low and you could sort of slump down. The bed also has really good slats with a bit of spring in them, the old ones were just solid lumps of wood. I don't know whether these have made the difference, because the expensive mattress suddenly feels a lot more comfortable and I feel as if I'm sleeping much better."

Cool it, guys

Another key factor affecting the sleeping environment is temperature. Again, it is essentially subjective, but there is general agreement among sleep researchers that lower temperatures are better. Your body temperature will drop as you sleep anyway, so if the room's temperature follows this pattern, you are less likely to be aware of the change and, therefore, wake up. Rooms that are too cold – below, say 15C – or too warm (22-23C or above) can affect the quality of sleep.

If you and your partner have different sensitivities to temperature, one of you may end up with a bad night sweating or shivering at the other's expense. If you're not quite ready for separate beds (or even separate rooms) you might at least consider separate duvets – this eliminates the nightly tug of war over the precious piece of fabric and allows both of you to choose your comfort level without affecting each other.

Sleeping by design

Q: How do you get a good night's sleep?

A: The conducive environment of a comfortable, welcoming bed and a restful, uncluttered room.

It should go without saying that the room we choose for sleep should be as clear and uncluttered as our minds. As we'll see in part three, the latter is rarely the case in the run up to bed, and the former isn't much cop either. In fact if we are being honest, most of us would own up to bedrooms that look like the back rooms of charity shops, with clothes and books strewn all over the place. But if you want to create a truly restful sleep environment you'll have to do better than that.

Robert Gray has already testified to the usefulness of Feng Shui as a protective measure in the bedroom, but the art of Feng Shui is customarily applied in its more traditional design based context to the benefit of the sleeper. While Feng Shui isn't the only theory behind bedroom design, the broad common sense of its philosophy of design has become increasingly adopted as part of wider interior design practice.

Much of what Feng Shui tells us about bedroom design is rooted in old-fashioned logic. The key areas in which this theory works in the bedroom include the physical and psychological impact of clutter, artwork, colour and positioning of the bed.

Utterly cluttered

We'll begin by looking at clutter – which is broadly defined as anything that is neither genuinely useful nor genuinely loved and cherished. I can picture hundreds of men whistling nervously and backing slowly out of the room at this point, but we are actually talking about inanimate objects here. Clutter also includes anything which is broken, unfinished or out of place.

Robert Gray feels that clutter is another area of harmful influence on life – akin to those invisible menaces of EMFs, microwaves and geopathic stress. His reasoning is as follows: "In my experience a cluttered home or office can dramatically affect the fortunes and well-being of the occupants. If a stream has become blocked and a stagnant pond has formed, there's no point in adding oxygen to the pond whilst the blockage is still in place. Clutter restricts the flow of healthy energy and stagnates the space that it's in. Getting rid of clutter can create a huge amount of positive energy in the body and can really help you to move forward into a brighter future.

"Looking at it from a common sense standpoint, clutter is very distracting and can remind you of all the things you need to do, which won't help you relax into a deep and restful sleep. Above all a clutter free bedroom is vital. Having an office in the bedroom (or even a work desk) is clutter for the mind. It is a constant reminder of the work that needs doing. For this reason, Feng Shui would advise against having a phone in the room. A TV can be quite stimulating right before sleep time which isn't conducive to slipping into a deep, restful sleep – it is also one of the most active (yang) objects in the house (bright, loud and distracting) and not at all recommended for your 'haven of peace' in the bedroom. Removing such clutter brings lightness and clarity to the mind, releases negative emotions and refreshes the spirit."

In short – be ruthless. Even those old heirlooms or souvenirs of long forgotten family holidays must have a purpose. Otherwise get them to the dump and get on with living in the present. Of course, once you've decided what to take out, you're confronted by the equally challenging task of what to put in its place. You should choose carefully, as Robert Gray advises: "The last impression we have as we close our eyes should be of a clear, tranquil space with positive, harmonious images around us. Artwork around the home can have a profound effect on us as we are constantly absorbing the imagery into our subconscious minds, so all artwork and ornaments should be peaceful and non-confrontational – the last thing you want to see before going to sleep is a picture of a bullfight or a poster of 'Terminator II'. Without the benefit of a Feng Shui consultation we cannot advise on specific positioning of artwork and ornaments as each is individually assessed based on the needs of the client, however good general advice is to ask: 'Do the images I see around me reflect the life I want for myself and specifically in the bedroom, are these images reflective of calm, peace and tranquillity?'."

So unless you're someone who finds bullfighting especially calming or you hanker after a career as a killer robot, it's worth trying to choose inspirational images like landscapes, images of natural beauty or simply a collection of reassuring colours.

Blues in the night

Colour plays a major part in a bedroom's suitability for sleep. It's a pretty subjective business, but there's an increasingly persuasive body of evidence that suggests colours directly influence our mood. This may be down to a variety of factors – ranging from an inescapable genetic predisposition to certain colours, to unconscious associations derived from our personal experience and from the collective unconscious, to conscious personal preference dictated by symbolic and cultural associations, to the more obvious trends and fashions of our age. Our reaction to any given colour may well be derived from a combination of any and all of the above. So it's easy to see why we all approach colour in different ways – which may well help to explain why your mother-in-law thought that dress went with those shoes.

But there are some broad rules of colour (even for mothers-in-law). Robert Gray explains more: "The human experience of colour is comprehensive, affecting both our physiological and psychological states. Red and blue have the greatest effect on physiology. Red represents fire in Feng Shui. It has been shown to be very stimulating to the brain and overuse can lead to excitability, anxiety, migraines, impatience and irritability. For this reason red should be treated with care (like fire), and used in smaller amounts to add zest where appropriate. By contrast the blue end of the spectrum, particularly violet at its far extreme, representing the water element, has a very calming effect on us and is particularly good for restful sleep.

"In a bedroom, be especially careful: I was called to a client's house as their son was sleeping quite badly. As a result, he was doing badly at school and his mood was quite irritable most of the time. When I entered his bedroom I was very surprised by the colour scheme. His favourite football team was Manchester United and the room was designed to match. His bedcover was a giant red flag, there were red posters all over the walls, many of the toys lying around were red and even his pyjamas were red! The advice was simple: dramatically reduce the amount of red in the room. They followed the advice and found that almost immediately he started sleeping much better."

As well as demonstrating the widely held belief among lovers of all things blue that supporting Manchester United is bad for your health, this story also helps us to establish some stricter rules for colour control in the bedroom. But it's not just the extremes of the spectrum that influence our moods, as Robert Gray continues: "The colour green represents the tree element and has been shown to stimulate creativity, optimism and ideas as well as bone growth and good posture. Earth tones (principally yellow, terracotta, pink and peach) provide supporting, nurturing influences and can also be quite restful as long as they are not too vivid. Yellow has been shown to enhance sociability and communication and reduce introspection and can therefore be a useful asset to reduce bickering. Yellow flowers are a classic Feng Shui cure for ongoing arguments. Overall, for a bedroom, avoid bright colours and strong patterns, go for muted tones and as a general rule the blue end of the spectrum is most restful."

Try out new positions

One of the principles of bedroom design that most people associate with Feng Shui is the positioning of the bed. Even within the ancient art, there's a few schools of thought about positioning, but one of the most common for determining the optimum position for the bed is based on the direction that the top of the head is facing when lying down. The eight main points of the compass are considered and the results, according to Robert Gray, are as follows:

North. Extremely still, deep, sleep. Quietens one's whole life.

North East. Unstable. Sharp, piercing energy, can lead to disturbed sleep and nightmares.

East. Spring-like energy: good for energy, ambition, starting things. Especially good for younger people.

South East. Similar to East but more subtle. Good for creativity and communication. Fine for sleep.

South. Far too active for sound sleep for most people. Can lead to too much fire in a relationship (i.e. arguments). The fire (like the colour red) can be too stimulating for sound sleep.

South West. South West/North East axis is unstable. More settled than the North East but can lead to overcaution.

West. Promotes relaxed contentment and romance. Quite good for relaxed sleep. Can lead to lack of motivation. Better for 'established' people.

North West. Promotes longer sleep, control, and leadership. Better for older people or people wanting more respect.

There are other factors to consider in terms of positioning. Robert Gray explains: "Try to position the bed so that you have full 'command of the room'. This means a good view of the door and window without being directly in front (as you enter the room) of either of them. Otherwise the subconscious part of your mind is always wary of intruders entering unannounced. Mirrors should be reduced to a minimum and shouldn't be positioned so that you can see yourself when relaxing in bed. This is said to either signify a third party or induce unpleasant dreams or disturbed sleep. Always have a headboard, which enhances feelings of security. If you have an en-suite bathroom or toilet keep the door closed to reduce the draining away of good energy.

"Try not to sleep under beams or sloping ceilings as this can cause sleepless nights and illness or, if the beam lies directly between the two of you, rifts between partners.

"Under each beam there is a subtle downward pressure which in Feng Shui terms is somewhat depressive."

Light and airy

While you're in the process of turning your bedroom into a sleep haven, you'll need to consider a couple more key issues – what do you do about lighting and how good is the air quality?

First of all, the lights – do you want to go for mood lighting, which can be great for romantic evenings, but bad for actually seeing anything when you want to get up and on with the day. Dimmer switches would be a great catch-all option – you can even buy these with a remote control, saving you the effort of getting out of bed to switch the light off before sleep.

Alternatively, use a selection of table lamps and/or standard lamps, with a bright central light used solely for the morning rush.

As we saw earlier, too much bright light is bad for sleeping, but it might be very good for waking. One new product you could try is a light clock, which steadily increases the amount of light in a room on the run-up to waking, allowing you to rouse naturally rather than to be ripped from sleep by a nagging alarm clock. These light clocks also work the other way, so if you have a child who won't go off to sleep without a light on, you can set the clock to gradually dim its light over a period of time.

Air quality is another fairly subjective issue – it's not something that most people will give serious thought to, but there's a fairly brisk trade in ionisers – machines which produce negative ions to counteract the surfeit of positive ions present in an indoor environment, while extracting harmful dust particles from the atmosphere. Too many positive ions lead to aggravation of allergies, stress and general feelings of fatigue among other complaints. In outdoor environments, these ions are in balance, so the ioniser 'freshens' the interior air to recreate the balance of outdoors. Or you could just open a window…

SLEEP DIARIES – BEDROOM DESIGN

ANNABEL: "My bedroom was really bright, four bold colours, one on each wall. Someone told me that my sleep problems might be related to these bright colours. It didn't make much sense as I figured my eyes would be closed and it would be dark at night anyway. But when I redecorated I decided to give it a go and went for better colours. They're certainly easier on the eye when I'm awake, but I don't think they've made a blind bit of difference."

CAROLE: "We moved house about a year ago and we never quite got around to emptying the boxes in our bedroom. The place was a pigsty, with clothes everywhere – every time I wanted to find something I had to search for ages, and I felt pretty awful seeing this mess first thing every morning. So when we finally got around to redecorating, I used some of the Feng Shui principles in the new design – I'd already used Feng Shui design to good effect in the garden, and I wanted to see how effective it could be in the house. We put all our clothes into a dressing room and turned the bedroom into a really luxurious area – we even bought a fancy new bed and opened up the fireplace to have a real fire. We replaced the awful, busy wallpaper with some pale greens and blues, like the colours of a calm sea, and these complemented the natural wood of our new bed. It gave the whole room a really 'organic' feel. I do sleep better, which must have something to do with the sense of achievement at finally getting the job done and picking up all the clutter, but it is so much nicer to wake up in this clean, clear room."

Security matters

Q: How do you get a good night's sleep?

A: Fit a good alarm system.

Ok, so we're straying beyond the hallowed territory of the bedroom here, but it is a rather depressing sign of the times that one major factor keeping us awake at night is the perceived threat to our home by burglars and intruders. All those night time bumps and creaks are extremely effective at working away at the overactive imagination in the worst possible way.

The solution may be exactly that outlined above – get a decent alarm system and remember to switch it on each night. At the very least it may pay to review the security of your home in general – check that you've got secure locks on garden gates, fit decent window and door locks. Use security lighting, lay gravel and plant a lot of prickly hedges in the garden to deter night time prowlers. Or you could even get a pet dog as these are useful guardians of the home and you can also blame them for all those unexplained nightly noises.

KEY POINTS

Keep intrusive light and noise to a minimum. Use sound proofing, blackout curtains or even earplugs and eye masks to lessen the impact of outside pollution.

Get rid of the gizmos. Clearing your bedroom of TVs, mobile phone chargers, computers and wireless networks can lower the likelihood of interference from electromagnetic fields. Avoid placing your bed against a wall with mains cables running through it.

Don't stress. If you're concerned that your room may be making you ill because of its geographic location, consult a geopathic stress consultant or a dowser.

Get comfortable. Make sure your bed is the right size and has the right level of support for your body. Get the best possible mattress, pillow and bed frame you can, and try them all before you buy.

Keep it cool. Your sleeping environment should avoid extremes of cold or warm – aim for an ambient temperature in the range of 18-21C.

Sleep by design. If you want your room to be restful, ensure it is free of clutter, use calming and restful artwork and avoid harsh, bright colours (especially red).

Low level lighting. When lighting the bedroom, you should think about its full range of functions. Use a dimmer switch or soft mood lighting (such as table lamps) to create a calm feel in the evenings, but make sure you have a bright main light for the morning pre-work rush.

Fresh air is good. Try to keep the room well ventilated if possible – if not, consider using an ioniser to improve air quality.

Feel secure. Outside of the bedroom, protect your house from intruders (and put your mind at rest) with improved security measures including window locks, defensive planting (thorny or sharp hedging) and external security lights.

PART THREE: In my head – the sleep routine

Q: How do you get a good night's sleep?

A: Simple and straightforward peace of mind.

Almost from the moment you wake in the morning you are preparing yourself for the following night's sleep. The things you eat and drink, the activities you choose and the thoughts you follow will all have vital parts to play when it comes to switching off the light and trying to rest at the end of the day. So how can you make sure the impact of all these elements is universally positive? In this section we'll look at a range of areas to consider, treatments to try and rules to adopt when planning the perfect pre-sleep routine. The areas we'll be considering in part three include:

★ diet – including food supplements

★ exercise and physical activity

★ relaxation tips including hypnotherapy and breathing techniques

★ aromatherapy

★ reflexology

★ massage

★ other alternative therapies – Ayurveda, Reiki, Shiatsu, music therapy, chiropractic, traditional Chinese medicine

★ the bedtime routine

Eat well, sleep well

Of all the issues surrounding sleeplessness, diet seems to be the one currently in vogue. The newspapers are full of stories about how a decent night's sleep keeps you young, sexy and, most of all, thin (which is a very positive spin on the alternative view that a bad night's sleep makes you eat comfort food). Poor sleep patterns in children are also believed to lead to poor diet.

Nutritional therapist Sally Child is the author of *The Art of Hiding Vegetables – sneaky ways to feed your children healthy food* (published by White Ladder Press, £7.99). She feels that there are some elemental causes for sleep problems that have a lot to do with what, when and how you choose to eat.

She says: "It's important to keep blood sugar steady through the night. When blood glucose drops, hormones are released, such as glucagon, cortisol, adrenaline and growth hormone. These hormones stimulate the brain which signals that it is time to eat – waking you up in the process. Good bedtime snacks to keep blood sugar steady include oatmeal and whole grain cereals, or a slice of wholemeal bread."

For some, the idea of a bedtime snack is a one-way ticket to indigestion hell. These poor souls might do better to adopt the maxim 'breakfast like a king, lunch like a lord, supper like a pauper'. Others may prefer to switch the focus of food from set mealtimes and instead snack at regular intervals five or six times a day. However you structure your diet, it's worth maintaining a broad balance of the wholegrain products mentioned above along with high energy fruits (bananas, dates, pineapple etc.) and vegetables like carrot and potato along with protein rich meat and fish. Try to think of food as the fuel to get your body through a normal, active day and a restful night.

Add the wrong fuel and the vehicle breaks down, and there are some fairly common dietary disasters that can have a major impact on sleep. Perhaps the most obvious of these is caffeine – used by many as a stimulant, it shouldn't require a rocket scientist to fathom that you will affect the quality of your sleep if you have a caffeinated drink close to bedtime.

What might come as a surprise, however, is just how long the effects of caffeine take to pass through the system. Sally Child recommends either eliminating caffeine from the diet altogether (no tea, coffee or caffeinated soft drinks) or limiting caffeine intake to the period prior to 4pm. That's around six or seven hours before bedtime for the average adult. Some nutritionists set the deadline even earlier, stating that any caffeinated drink taken after mid-morning may have an impact on the following night's rest. If you can't sleep without a hot cup of something, try a milky drink like Ovaltine, green tea, or even better – if you can stand the somewhat acquired taste – camomile tea, which is also said to have a soporific effect. If you'd rather avoid the sensation of drinking a hedgerow, you could always stick a spoonful of honey in with it as the natural sugars in pure honey may also help to keep you from waking.

Alcohol is another stimulant, as are recreational drugs, including the nicotine found in cigarettes – and all of these should be avoided late at night.

While some people claim they need an alcoholic 'night-cap' to fall asleep – and almost 40 per cent of our survey respondents said they drink alcohol in the hour before bed – the likelihood is that this drink is merely acting as a mild sedative, producing only light sleep. The drinker may wake in the middle of the night feeling dehydrated and not sufficiently refreshed.

As we age, it's tempting to avoid all drinks prior to bed so that we can try to get through the night without having to get up for a toilet trip. But, as Sally Child explains, cutting fluid intake altogether is counter productive, as the sleeper will wake anyway, but with a feeling of dehydration or a headache instead.

The better bet is to adopt a similar approach to fluid intake as that recommended above for food – little and often. Six to eight half-pint glasses of water drunk throughout the day, with the final glass drunk shortly before bed, should keep the body sufficiently hydrated all night.

The hormone serotonin, which helps to regulate sleep, may be stimulated by certain types of food that are rich in a substance called tryptophan. These include cereals, milk, cottage cheese, bananas and even turkey, which might go some way towards explaining why everyone always falls asleep immediately after Christmas lunch.

It's also possible to supplement your diet to encourage production of serotonin. Sally Child explains: "Taking 50mg of vitamin B6 may help by increasing serotonin. This hormone may also be raised by taking 5 H-T-P (100mg). The effect of this supplement may be enhanced if taken with carbohydrate, and you also need to ensure that B6, B3 and magnesium levels are maintained when taking this as these help convert 5 H-T-P to serotonin.

"In addition, if you have low magnesium or calcium levels, taking supplements may help muscle relaxation, as these are calming minerals. Finally, B complex vitamins, especially B6 and B12 can be effective against sleeping problems within days."

Asphalia – the grass is greener?

One food supplement that's causing a major stir among advocates of alternative and herbal remedies is Asphalia. This treatment, supplied in powder or capsule form, is a combination of grain products, leaves, garden vegetables and berries, rich in natural antioxidants, which counter the ageing and damaging effects on the body of free radicals – atoms with an unpaired set of electrons which can attack the body's cell structure in the search for electrons.

The reason that this supplement has been hailed by some as a breakthrough in natural sleep treatments is that it contains a low dose of melatonin, the body's own antioxidant, which in this case is extracted from plants. This ingredient is intended to compensate for the lowering of natural melatonin generation in later life, and to counter the alleged reduction of human melatonin production caused by interference from electromagnetic fields.

Melatonin supplements have traditionally been viewed with

deep suspicion by clinicians, nutritionists and herbalists alike, and Asphalia cannot be marketed as a melatonin supplement, as these are unlicensed in the UK. But Asphalia, shrewdly named after the ancient Greek word for safety, is the result of a new approach which seems to be winning some fairly strong backing.

The product was created by biologist Roger Coghill, who explains the theory behind Asphalia: "The human body is not prepared for alternating electrical fields. Our brains cannot distinguish between these fields and natural light, so they have the same effect, which is to suppress the natural production of melatonin. Around ten years ago, it was discovered that plants contain melatonin and that it does the same job as that produced by animals. Our breakthrough was finding out that the pharmacological level of melatonin delivery – in the tablets commercially available in the US – is a massive overdose, it's not dangerous, but it's not helpful either. Our melatonin is delivered at a much lower physiological level, using the richest melatonin producing plant available."

Roger Coghill's claims are impressive, and the names lining up to endorse his product – including natural health supremo Jan De Vries – make for persuasive reading. Perhaps the most compelling fact about the product's apparent benefits comes from the fact that it is without obvious side effects, a rare claim among sleep treatments.

Roger Coghill adds: "It's a phenomenal sleep improver, as it doesn't damage the sleep architecture and doesn't disturb REM sleep. Everyone above the age of 50 ought to be taking this on a regular basis."

Whether Asphalia is truly the miracle product that its creator claims will ultimately be measured in its take-up and success. But Roger Coghill stresses that he's making no bold claims to have discovered a method of treating chronic sleep disorders. He adds: "The scientific support for what I'm saying is strong, but Asphalia is helpful only for sleep disturbance among healthy people."

SLEEP DIARIES – DIET

ANNABEL: "I have taken some of the dietary advice into consideration, like snacking before sleep. I have always done this, but now I think more carefully about what I eat. I think it helps as I need less, which is good for me and yet it keeps me going through the night."

DEAN: "I've always suffered terribly from indigestion and acid at night if I eat late, so I didn't feel I could go for a late snack. I did start eating a larger meal at lunchtime and then just having a sandwich on whole-grain bread in the evening. This made a huge difference in terms of cutting time spent awake with indigestion pains. But I reckon the biggest change has come from cutting caffeine from my routine. I'm a real tea drinker, I'm used to about eight cups a day. Now I have one cup in the morning and one in the afternoon and that's my lot. I don't drink alcohol after 9pm either, and I must have cut the incidences of waking with a headache almost completely. Before, I'd wake with a dehydration headache every other day, now I get one or two a month. It must have helped my sleep too, because I feel a lot better in myself."

Warm up, wind down

Q: How do you get a good night's sleep?

A: Physical tiredness always works for me. I notice that it takes me longer to nod off if it's a day when I haven't had my hour plus of exercise in the morning.

It's hard to write these words without the feeling that I've been possessed by the spirit of my grandmother, but getting outside and doing some physical activity really could be good for you. The theory is fairly simple – exercise lets us know that we are awake, increasing the body's flow of the 'happy hormone' endorphin. It makes us feel invigorated, raises our body temperature and increases our heart rate. All these are good for making you feel alive and energised.

If you exercise outdoors, or in a well lit environment, you're also ensuring that your brain isn't secreting melatonin and making you drowsy. You're getting fresh air and, if you exercise hard enough, you'll probably feel physically tired at the end of the session. So it's all good news, right?

Up to a point. Exercise, like every part of the pre-sleep routine, has a specific place and shouldn't just be used as a replacement for a sleeping tablet – i.e. don't knock yourself out just before bed with a hundred sit-ups. In fact, don't do any strenuous exercise just before bed – all the positive benefits of exercise outlined above would keep you stimulated and wide awake long into the night. There's no clearly defined optimum time to exercise, but it's logical to assume that an energy boost around teatime is a good way to build you up before you begin the long wind down to sleep.

If you've had a long and sedentary day at work, exercise is a great way of getting you through the evening without dropping off on the train home, or on the sofa once you get there.

So what kind of exercise is best and how often should you exercise? The best exercises for boosting energy are gentle aerobic exercises like walking and swimming as well as those that you might do in a gym or health club – treadmill jogging and static cycling being the most popular and accessible. In an ideal world you should try to exercise every day for around half an hour, but if that's not possible then three to four times a week will suffice.

The physical downside to excessive exercise is the possibility that you wake in the night with aches, twinges and cramps caused by overexertion. It's clearly important to start gently – and to consult a qualified fitness instructor before beginning any exercise regime. Remember to always do some gentle stretches to help you warm up and warm down, this is vital to prevent muscle strains.

Further gentle stretches, in the form of yoga, Pilates, tai chi, or the wind down stretches from your fitness routine, can be beneficial nearer bedtime, both to lessen the likelihood of muscle twinges in the night and to create a general mood of rest and relaxation.

And finally, another underestimated form of relaxing and (hopefully) pleasurable exercise is sex. Love making that's extremely energetic and vigorous carries the same risks as other frenetic activity near bedtime, but gentle, calm and enjoyable sex is just about the nicest way to switch off from the cares of the world and relax into the arms of the one you love. Or at least that's the average man's excuse for rolling over and passing out. But seriously, it's a perfectly valid form of exercise and anything that contributes to a general sense of well-being puts you in a better place for sleep.

Relax (don't do it)

Q: How do you get a good night's sleep?

A: My secret of good sleep is to respect it rather than regarding it as a nuisance between now and tomorrow. Make a bit of space to let everything calm down. I use meditation and relaxation a lot rather than just going from full-on and then expecting to go to bed and sleep.

It isn't easy, but there is one broad principle that sleep researchers, and our surveyed sleepers, agree upon – the best sleep routine is one that leaves you relaxed at bedtime. That might sound blindingly obvious, but in a world where people go straight to bed after battling zombies on their game stations, or after fighting a different kind of war against other bidders on auction websites, or even watching the latest adrenaline pumping action TV show, relaxation can come at a premium. So have we forgotten how to wind down?

Homeopath Andrew Kirk certainly thinks so. In fact he feels that a hectic life might not simply be bad for our sleep pattern, it could be seriously damaging to our health.

He explains: "One of the things which I feel is very underrated is the way in which society in general is geared up to raising adrenaline levels until this becomes a chronic state – adverts; fast moving, jump cut TV shows; loud music. As a result of all this, people's nervous systems are overstimulated. They are going around with their adrenals pumped up and that will cause disturbances, uneasiness, restless sleep, even without any other trigger.

"There was a story in the news a few weeks ago arguing that we make too much fuss about stress, and that it is an evolutionary mechanism designed for our benefit – and that's all well and good if you're climbing a tree while being chased by a tiger – but what they missed out was that it's not supposed to be there all the time. Our systems don't get a chance to calm down, the excess adrenaline stays in the system and poisons it, so you get all kinds of other problems as well."

This view of an imbalanced society – a culture that is incompatible with the concept of relaxation – is firmly endorsed by hypnotherapist Glenn Harrold, whose self-help CDs are international bestsellers, and who feels that our complex relationship with sleep owes a lot to the intellectual demands of modern life.

He says: "Everything about the way we live now is so fast and furious that when it comes to switching off at night, it becomes difficult because your mind is so stimulated. It's been said that we make more decisions in a week than our grandparents did in a year. When you're in your left brain intellectual mind and you've been making decisions all day it can be very hard to let your right brain take over at night and guide you into that sleep state."

This, according to Glenn Harrold, is where his style of hypnotherapy kicks in. Combining skilled hypnotherapy techniques with state-of-the-art digital recording technology, Glenn's CDs aim to guide the listener into a relaxed state of mind then, using a mixture of hypnotic echoed background vocals and original music, the listener is lulled into sleep. That's the theory at least, and to be fair it has proved to be very successful indeed. Glenn is the UK's biggest selling self-help audio author and a member of the British School of Clinical Hypnosis, one of the country's most respected clinical hypnotherapy organisations.

He adds: "I wanted to try and cover every psychological reason why people would struggle to fall asleep. It's about giving people suggestions while they are in a trance that they will respond to afterwards. The CDs help to take you from the left brain analytical thinking into right brain creative, daydreaming, relaxed thinking. To get to sleep your brainwaves need to slow down from beta to alpha and beyond and the CDs help to bridge that gap. For full effect, you should be lying down in bed with headphones on. Suggestions pan from the left to right hemisphere on the stereo range."

The pride that Glenn takes in the technical precision of his CDs is something that harks back to his days as a musician, but they aren't simply designed to be something pleasant to listen to, they have a place in a wider relaxation routine, as he explains: "It's about conditioning and creating the right environment, but it's also about getting into a healthy sleep pattern – if you are stuck in that rut where you're not going to bed at a regular time and you're up all hours, the body does respond to that. If you develop a routine, your brain and body get used to you switching off at a particular time, so you wake up earlier and brighter. I guess the CD is very good at helping you get back into that habit."

Of course, some habits are hard to break, and Glenn freely admits that hypnotherapy CDs and self-hypnosis have limited applications for more serious disorders.

He explains: "It does tend to be about the individual – with hypnosis CDs in general, if you take 10 people and they're all using the CD, two or three have dramatic improvements, three or four a good improvement, and the remainder get nothing from them. There could be other issues involved. I've worked with clients one-to-one who've had an experience in the middle of the night that's caused trauma. That memory has become repressed and they've developed a fear of going to bed in their adult life, but they don't make the connection. In that case a CD wouldn't make a difference, they'd need a one-to-one therapy session to get to the root cause."

But he's had plenty of success stories, and the most satisfying are those which come from people who've previously given up all hope of a meaningful solution. "Sometimes there's the classic scenario that the CD is used as a last resort. I had a lovely email from someone who's been on sleeping tablets for 40 years and my CD got her off the tablets."

With or without his CDs to guide you, Glenn Harrold is a firm advocate of creating a dedicated 'space' in your routine to down-shift from your busy day to a relaxed night.

He adds: "As a rule, if you practise a self-hypnosis session before bed, or in bed, you can take your mind away from the day's thoughts and actually slow it down and prepare in the best possible way to go off to sleep. There's always a pay-off to the busy lifestyle, if you're multitasking throughout the day you need to balance it out with other activities that take you away from that, yoga, meditation, self-hypnosis. If you carry on living at 100 miles an hour something will have to give."

SLEEP DIARIES – HYPNOTHERAPY CD

ANNABEL: "I listened to the CD and as embarrassed as I am to say this, it kind of scared me. One of my friends can normally sleep but has gone through a stage of not sleeping so I gave it her for a night and she is now back to sleeping like a baby. So I know it's just me. I'm not sure what it is, I can see how it is relaxing and when I'm listening to it during the day (just to see what it's like) I'm fine. But it's a scary feeling being alone and awake and the voice seemed less relaxing. I find it hard to explain just why the CD was scary and I have to confess I think part of it is actually the fear that it may work – after all these years of not sleeping I'm a little scared of what it would be like."

EMILY: *"When I started using it I spent some time feeling very silly listening to it. I got quite critical. But having said that I don't think I actually heard the end of it, even on the first night. The effect was immediate. I've only heard the end three times and I've used it most nights for a couple of months. A couple of times I've gone to bed thinking I'm not going to use it and I laid there thinking shall I or shan't it switch it on? In the end I put it on and it worked. There's been a couple of times I've gone to bed and haven't used it, not really consciously. But I've woken up the next day a bit freaked out because I've actually slept through the night. I remembered everything that was in the CD. It talks you into a routine. Now, when I go to bed, I sleep. For me to wake up the next morning without having moved in bed, that is a bizarre feeling."*

FRANCES: *"I'm afraid the CD didn't make a huge difference to my sleep pattern. It did make me feel relaxed and quite soporific though, so that was good, although I can't really switch out my light and go to sleep unless I've read, so I found myself switching off the CD, taking the headphones off and picking up my book, then reading for another 20 minutes or so, by which point I'd usually nod off. So I'm not sure how much of an effect it had on me really."*

As Glenn Harrold himself says, hypnotherapy is not the only relaxation technique available to the sleeper. In fact, relaxation for better sleep isn't solely restricted to bedtime, as a generally calm and relaxed demeanour can help you get through the day without the sharp peaks and troughs of stress that may add up to a troubled mind.

There's a range of meditations, relaxation tips and breathing techniques to try – many of which encourage the individual to focus on a specific event that makes them happy and calm, or on a physical process like tensing and then relaxing muscles. It doesn't matter which method you choose, it's more important to find something that you're completely comfortable with, that fits into your daily routine and provides you with the space and the intensity of focus to lift your mind away from the issues of the day and into the calm of the night.

Another great advantage of finding a relaxation technique that works well for you is the ease with which you can use this if you happen to wake in the night. Knowing that you have a planned response to unexpected waking can be a huge asset, especially for light sleepers who find it hard to switch off from outside noises.

SLEEP DIARY: RELAXATION TECHNIQUES

BARBARA: "I actually started off by using a CD, but found it quite awkward to wear the headphones and didn't want to wake my husband, so in the end I just adapted some of the things the man on the CD was saying – about deep breathing and focusing on a specific place or event. The breathing techniques in particular are useful – I've not been doing them for long, but I can really see this working for me in the future."

CAROLE: "I've been taught one specific technique that is now working brilliantly for me in times of real stress. It goes something like this: Lie on your back with your arms relaxed by your sides, palms facing upwards. Let every muscle in your body relax. Then concentrate on your heels, imagining that they are incredibly heavy, pushing themselves down into the mattress. Work you way slowly and methodically up your body – ankles, calves, knees etc. – right up to the top of your head, which you visualise pressing hard into the pillow. Of course, the idea is that you never get as far as this, and in all honesty I've rarely got all the way through the technique without dropping off. I don't really know why it works, but focusing on a very simple, specific task, and relaxing my body at the same time always seems to do the job for me."

The sweet smell of success

Q: How do you get a good night's sleep?

A: I use lavender oil, just a few drops on my pillow and in the bath, and I find this is a great help. The smell is incredibly comforting and soothing.

We've seen that learning to relax and shut out the cares of the day is crucial for a good sleep routine. But it's not always easy to focus the mind on what you should be doing. That's where a certain sense of ceremony surrounding the sleep routine can come in – something that is unique to night time, and that makes you feel special, comforted and calm. We're talking aromatherapy.

It seems that everyone knows a little about aromatherapy, of all the alternative and complementary therapies it's the one that's most easily absorbed into a busy routine, but as with any other treatment it only becomes effective when its is fully understood and properly implemented.

So let's start with a bit of background. Aromatherapy is the broad term for the use of essential oils, which are essences created from the distilled extracts of plants. These have been used as treatments for more than 5,000 years and are said to have innumerable healing properties. Though they are not toxic, oils in their undiluted form are incredibly powerful and most should never be directly applied to the skin. Instead, essential oils are commonly used in the following ways: in the bath, in a burner, on a bulb ring (a porous ring that fits over a light bulb and is gently warmed, giving off the aroma of the essential oil) or in a vaporiser. They can also be used on a pillow or a tissue and simply inhaled.

Oils can be blended – two or three oils working together is common, though you should use no more than four as a maximum. Each oil is intended to treat a specific complaint.

One of the most common applications of essential oils is through the medium of aromatherapy massage. In a massage, essential oils are diluted within a safe carrier oil like Sweet Almond Oil and applied directly to the skin using a series of movements and strokes designed to ease tension, relieve pain and balance the emotions.

So how do essential oils work? When they are inhaled, essential oils go to work on the olfactory system, encouraging the release of endorphins and a general feeling of well-being. Oils applied to the skin are absorbed into the blood stream and muscle tissue, through the organs and ultimately to the excretory system. They don't remain in the body for long, but they are said to cleanse and relax as they pass through.

Essential oils used as sleep remedies are chosen for their sedative and relaxing properties. They include lavender, which is perhaps the best known and most widely available sleep promoting essential oil, but also camomile, marjoram and neroli. Each of these oils is said to calm, soothe and relieve anxiety. In common with most essential oils, they also have antiseptic qualities.

How safe are essential oils? Any treatment that is powerful enough to positively affect your mood is also potentially harmful if misused. There's a number of issues relating to essential oils that you must bear in mind before trying these remedies. If you suffer from high blood pressure you are advised to avoid using oils like rosemary, sage and thyme because, as well as making you smell like the Sunday roast, these oils stimulate the circulatory system. Pregnant women are advised to avoid essential oils until they reach the final trimester. In fact, if you suffer from any medical condition, you're better off consulting a qualified aromatherapist before trying any oils.

A vast range of oils is available to buy over the counter in their pure state or as part of a massage blend. If you're planning to use oils for massage in the home and you want to make up your own blend, aim to dilute the essential oils to around 2.5-3 per cent of the total solution. If you're using essential oils neat, eight drops will suffice in a bath, and four to six drops are all you'll need on a burner, bulb ring, vaporiser or on a tissue for inhaling. Don't be tempted to use more in an effort to increase the effects of the aroma as this won't work. If in doubt, consult an aromatherapist or do your research first – there are many good books available on aromatherapy techniques, there's even a whole book devoted to the sleep inducing lavender oil.

So what's the best way to incorporate aromatherapy into the sleep routine? Many people feel that a bath is a good prelude to sleep – preferably taken around an hour before bed – as the warm water relaxes muscle tension and raises body temperature, which then drops naturally to dovetail with bedtime, rendering you relaxed and sleepy. Supporting your bathtime routine with essential oils helps to promote this feeling of winding down at the end of the day. Experts advise that you should burn some oils in the bedroom while you bathe, so that when you're finished, the comforting, calming aroma is carried through into the bedroom.

Aromatherapy is a big business, and if you're keen to explore the reported health benefits of essential oils and aromatherapy massage, there are clinics throughout the country offering specialist consultations and treatments that are tailored to individual requirements – it's even possible to get a qualified aromatherapy masseur to visit your house shortly before bedtime to gently rub you to sleep. While a one-off massage is a perfectly worthwhile experience, experts recommend a course of repeat treatments over a matter of weeks or months to give the full effect.

Fancy footwork

Reflexology is allied to aromatherapy and massage in the sense that it works on the circulatory system and aims to reduce tension and stress. It is also possible to combine the disciplines in a reflexology massage using essential oils. But what makes reflexology different from these other treatments is the extraordinary way in which it focuses on reflex points on the hands or feet to treat symptoms that manifest themselves on a different and seemingly unrelated part of the body.

Of course, the reflexology expert would argue that they are entirely related, explaining that the body is divided into longitudinal zones in which energy flows from the feet upwards. By massaging a particular part of the foot, the practitioner can identify imbalances and treat problems. Rather like an aromatherapy massage, reflexology is useful for the sleep routine as it can help to relieve tension and stress, as well as muscular problems. With some prior knowledge of the reflex points, it is possible to do your own reflexology massage, so again it may be beneficial to incorporate this into the late night routine.

SLEEP DIARIES – AROMATHERAPY, MASSAGE AND REFLEXOLOGY

EMILY: *"I had a friend who was learning aromatherapy massage and used me as a guinea pig. She had some fantastic smelling oils. It was pleasant, but I think I was too aware of what she was doing and that stopped me from relaxing. I've also used lavender oil and camomile oil on my pillow. It's a very acquired smell, but boy did it knock me out. It worked well for a couple of weeks, but then I got used to the smell and stopped believing it was going to work. Hot baths with the oil helped to make me feel sleepy, but again these stopped working after a while."*

BARBARA: *"I got hold of some lavender essential oil and tried it in my bath for a week – then had another week trying it on my pillow. Unfortunately it made no difference to my sleep pattern at all – I still woke at least once each night."*

CAROLE: *"I had a reflexology massage, just as a one-off to see what it was like. First thing I'd say is that it was incredibly relaxing – with a normal massage there's the worry about stripping off and not being comfortable, but with someone working on my feet alone, I could wear what I want, and I wasn't so self-conscious. Afterwards I felt really good, but then there was the drive home, and by the time I got to bed some of the benefit had worn off. That being said, I was more relaxed going to bed and I went off to sleep well. I'd definitely consider doing it again, but I think it would work better as a course of treatments."*

Massage received and understood

Q: How do you get a good night's sleep?

A: I am undergoing holistic massage therapy to try and relax my body and ease the tension in my muscles, particularly my neck and shoulders. I've only had a couple of sessions, but I find I am able to sleep well following the therapy.

Away from the soothing strokes of aromatherapy massage, the more structured discipline of massage (and sports massage) also has a role to play in promoting a good sleep pattern. Qualified massage therapist Zoë Archer has treated a range of patients with serious muscular problems, and she feels that massage has a major role to play in general well-being, and in improving sleep in particular.

She explains: "I've had some great results with people who have sleep problems. I've treated people at 8pm and they've slept brilliantly through the next two nights. For people with muscle disorders, a massage before bed just relaxes the muscles enough to ease their concerns. I treated somebody with Parkinson's Disease and the muscle tremors he used to get would keep him awake at night. He'd always get a good night's sleep after a massage. Massage is a very powerful thing which is also very underrated. I've treated people with ME and MS, and massage for these people showed marked difference in pain levels and overall well-being, which helped them sleep and improved their general condition."

If you feel that massage is an area that you'd like to explore, it may be possible to arrange an NHS referral through your GP. Though services vary from area to area, it is worth getting in touch with your doctor's practice to find out more.

Best of the rest cures

There's a whole industry of alternative therapies that claim to offer positive benefit to the sleeper, mainly through relaxation and destressing. We'll take a look at some of the more mainstream approaches in part four, but here's a run-down of some other therapies and their main messages:

Ayurveda. This is a traditional Indian holistic form of treatment dating back more than 5,000 years. The emphasis of Ayurveda is on prevention rather than cure, as it aims to keep a balance of three vital forces at work within each of us. These forces, or doshas, are called Vata, Pitta and Kapha. According to Ayurveda, our personality is determined by which of these doshas is dominant in our make-up. In an ideal world, our doshas are all working in harmony to promote complete health – in reality, there is often an imbalance, which is what Ayurveda seeks to redress.

Feng Shui consultant Robert Gray draws on the principles of Ayurveda for his work. He explains: "My clients who suffer poor sleep for environmental reasons either sleep very heavily and feel dreadful the next day or they can't get to sleep, or if they do, they wake frequently. I can predict which category people will fall into based on their dosha type as defined by the ancient holistic health model of Ayurveda (Ayus meaning life and Veda roughly translating as knowledge). As a general principle those with a strong Vata score will find difficulty in getting to sleep whilst those with a strong Kapha score will tend to sleep through but find it very difficult to rise. However a challenging sleeping environment will accentuate these characteristics further."

Reiki. This treatment originated in Japan in the early 20th century. It involves channelling the body's energy to re-establish harmony and balance. Practitioners, known as Reiki masters, use their hands a few centimetres above the patient's body, manipulating the energy field from outside. Though some elements of Reiki also involve touch, it is the control of this invisible energy that allows the Reiki master to restore equilibrium in the individual. Does it work? It's anyone's guess, but there's a growing band of followers, and a positive legion of Reiki Masters in the UK alone. If nothing else, Reiki shows that the power of human touch can be immensely relaxing and restful.

Shiatsu. This is another form of massage, also originating from the far east, but which is much more focused on touch and pressure than Reiki. A Shiatsu massage involves pressure applied by the masseur to various 'acupoints' around the body. The aim of Shiatsu is also to correct imbalances in the body's essential energy. Shiatsu is a slightly less controversial treatment than Reiki, as it shares common roots with other mainstream therapies like reflexology and acupuncture.

Music therapy. This is a simple yet underrated form of relaxation therapy. From classical music to whale song to the sound of the ocean lapping at the shore, it doesn't really matter what you choose – though you might steer away from heavy metal or thumping techno beats – as long as the music has the desired effect of helping you drift from wakefulness to sleep.

Chiropractic. Though not a treatment aimed directly at the sleeper, chiropractic claims to be able to provide relief for people who suffer from back, neck and shoulder pain using gentle manipulation techniques on joints, the spine and muscles where there is restricted movement.

Traditional Chinese Medicine. This broad term describes a whole range of treatments derived from ancient Chinese Taoist thinking. These include acupuncture, which we'll come back to in more detail in part four. The general philosophy behind Traditional Chinese Medicine (TCM) is holistic – treating the whole person rather than the specific complaint. In this philosophy body and mind are united and each informs the other. Another popular form of therapy that exists under the umbrella of TCM is the breathing exercise therapy known as qigong, which aims to promote balance and harmony in the individual.

Time for some discipline?

It's a truism that the bedroom should only be used for sleep and sex, but like all truisms, this one is grounded in fact. What you do in bed is just as important as what you do before bed.

An incredible 56 per cent of the sleepers surveyed for this book regularly work or use their computers in the bedroom just before switching out the light. Some people regard this time as an important download for the thoughts and issues that need to be handled in the morning. But if you're trying to turn the bedroom into a sanctuary of sleep you need to make a greater effort to put distance between your work and your relaxation. If you have unresolved work issues, you're better off trying to shut them out using relaxation techniques or self-hypnosis than by trying to deal with them all before sleeping. If you're worried about waking in the night with a crucial thought, keep a pad and pen or a memo recorder by the bed.

We've already seen in part two that televisions in the bedroom are a bad idea – but this is not solely because of the adrenaline rush that the idiot box can give, it's also because TV is an ever present temptation when waking in the night. Having a computer on hand for some late night surfing is equally damaging to the brain's efforts to rest and calm down. Even reading is of questionable benefit to sleepers, though many people would not do without their nightly chapter. In short, it's easier to focus on sleep with fewer distractions around, and it's easier to get back to sleep when waking in an environment without many external stimuli.

Even in this pared down haven of sleep, there's the inside of your head to cope with. If something's on your mind, if you just don't feel able to sleep for any reason and you've been lying awake for anything up to half an hour, you should get up.

You must regard your bed as a place for sleep, if it takes on other connotations you may be heading for serious problems, as Professor Kevin Morgan of the University of Loughborough's Sleep Research Centre explains: "If there's one thing that insomniacs do it's learn to be awake in bed. People with insomnia spend more time in bed than people without sleep problems. It's part of the problem. They learn that their bed is something they stay awake in and repeatedly reinforce this. Most of us, without a sleep problem, spend about 95 per cent of our time in bed asleep. With a sleep problem, about 30 per cent of the time is awake. That's extremely unhealthy, so getting out of bed is a training device, teaching your body that the bed is something you sleep in not stay awake in."

Getting out of bed, making a hot drink, reading or just sitting in another room – preferably without the stimulation of a TV or computer – can allow you to break an unhelpful association. Then when you're ready to return to bed, you're more likely to relax into sleep.

Making changes to your sleep environment and developing a more formal and effective pre-sleep routine can help to improve quality of sleep for many healthy people. But sadly that's not the full story of sleeplessness. Insomnia and sleep disorders blight lives and cause considerable suffering to everyone affected. In the following sections we'll take a look at some of the more common disorders as well as discussing the principal areas of treatment for insomnia.

KEY POINTS

Eat for sleep. Treat food as the fuel to get you through to the next day – you need slow release energy food to ensure that you don't wake hungry in the night. Don't eat too late or you'll battle indigestion all night. Many people find that five or six snack meals spread over the day are better for keeping energy levels up than three big meals.

Get active, but not too active. Don't do any strenuous exercise too close to bedtime – anything that stimulates the mind and body will make sleep harder to come by. Instead, focus your exercise regime on late afternoon, with around half an hour of aerobic exercise daily.

Calm down. Use relaxation techniques, breathing exercises or hypnotherapy to switch your mind and body from the frantic pace of life into a calmer, more relaxed pre-sleep zone. Yoga and meditation are great ways to clear the mind and create a more peaceful environment.

Smell good. Use aromatherapy to complement your 'calm zone', reinforcing the sense of ceremony around bedtime with calming and sedating oils like lavender and camomile.

Use aromatherapy oils in a bath around an hour before bed to relax your muscles and raise your body's temperature prior to winding down to sleep.

The gentle touch. Use techniques such as reflexology and massage to ease aching muscles and work off stress and tension. If you can get someone to give you a massage shortly before bed, that's great – but self-massage can be effective too.

Natural rhythm. Establish a bedtime routine and stick to it. Don't lie awake in bed for longer than half an hour at a time – if you can't sleep, get up and do something calming and relaxing – read a book, listen to some restful music. Try to avoid watching TV or using a computer in bed, or just prior to sleep.

PART FOUR: A serious business – insomnia treatments

In this section we'll take a look at the main options available to the insomniac who goes to his or her doctor and requests help in managing the condition. We'll also consider treatment options from a very different, and more controversial, perspective.

We'll be looking at the following treatments for insomnia:

★ sleeping pills/pharmaceutical treatments

★ talking therapies – specifically Cognitive Behavioural Therapy

★ alternative therapies – acupuncture, homeopathy, herbal medicine

Insomnia is a tough challenge to face and the sufferer currently has fairly limited options in terms of mainstream, free of charge treatment on the NHS. In fact, if you go to your doctor with a complaint of excessive sleeplessness you are likely to be given a lecture on sleep hygiene and then offered a course of sleeping tablets for a period of anything up to six months. But does this mean your GP has no viable alternatives, or just that you're in the wrong place for treatment?

In the opinion of Professor Kevin Morgan of the University of Loughborough's Sleep Research Centre, it's a little bit of both. He feels that one of the central problems facing the effective treatment of insomnia is that GPs simply don't have the enthusiasm and level of expertise for the subject. He says: "The problem with insomnia in the UK healthcare system is that it's an abandoned child. General Practice primarily treats it. Sometimes they treat it badly and don't want to get involved at all.

"So the question is whether the medical profession is the right territory? Medicine has maintained a proprietorial relationship to sleep and its dysfunctions for a long time now. Insomnia is one of those areas that it really should let go of because its interest and influence hasn't been very helpful. It's engendered an attitude toward the management of insomnia that renders the individual who experiences it totally passive, then introduces clinical responses, mainly sleeping drugs, that over the last thirty years have made the situation substantially worse not better."

If you close your eyes and spin around in a circle with your arms extended, you're more likely to wallop someone critical of sleeping pills than an advocate. If you tried the same thing 20 years ago, the reverse may well have happened. Sleeping pills have developed a stigma that is borne out of their overuse and overprescription, but it is not necessarily a fair or balanced depiction of their usefulness.

The main criticisms aimed at sleeping pills are as follows: they don't treat the source of insomnia, they simply mask its effects; they don't induce natural, restful sleep, they reduce the patient to unconsciousness; they contain many potentially hazardous and disturbing side effects; it is easy to become dependent and to effectively destroy your ability to sleep naturally.

In a court of law you'd have to fear for this defendant. But then sleeping pills don't pretend to deny any of the above – read the user's information leaflet for popular pharmaceutical sleeping treatments like Mogadon and you'll find advice and clarifications regarding all of the above. It's made clear that these pills do not address insomnia, they merely provide a window of relief from its effects. They are an effective final line of defence for people who have become too incapacitated by sleep deprivation to cope. They are not miraculous, you will not sleep better as a consequence of taking them, you'll probably feel a bit groggy (at best) after using them and you will pay a heavy penalty for excessive or prolonged use. All of this is laid out for the user to read and act upon.

The problem comes back to the point of delivery – are GPs discriminating effectively between people who need sleeping pills as a temporary escape from the debilitating effects of chronic insomnia and those who simply want a better night's sleep because they've got exams coming up? Equally, are they making effective efforts to follow up the short term prescription of sleeping pills with a genuine attempt to address the root cause of insomnia?

The answer is probably no in both instances, but not because GPs are necessarily lazy or indifferent towards insomnia. Patients play a key role in the demands they make and the lengths they are prepared to go to in order to deal with their problem. Sleeping pills are not a magic 'cure' for sleep problems, and they should never be viewed in this way. They do, however, have a role to play in sleep management, and if you're confident that you can keep your usage under control, they can be extremely effective as a way of correcting a temporary disturbance in a sleep pattern – but only for a couple of days. In other words, if you're just after a quick fix, you'll get one, but pills won't provide what you need beyond the very short term.

A consequence of the limited help offered by the GP is a general reluctance on the part of patients to take their sleep problems to a health professional – possibly for fear of being pushed into a course of drugs. According to the national average, around 20 to 25 per cent of the sleepers surveyed for this book will have significant sleep problems, and yet as few as 12 per cent have actually sought medical advice for their condition – and half of these were disappointed with the advice they received.

A major part of this problem is perceived choice. For a number of reasons, which we'll discuss in more depth later, the GP has an overwhelming bias in favour of pharmaceutical remedies. This suggests that there's little in the way of viable alternatives for treatment of insomnia on the NHS, which is untrue. So what are these alternatives, how do they work and how can patients access them?

Now you're talking

Cognitive Behavioural Therapy (CBT) for insomnia is about as far removed from sleeping pills as a treatment can be. Rather than offering a short term quick fix, this psychological treatment – one of a collection of so-called 'talking therapies' – aims to teach people how to structure their thoughts and approach the anxieties and fears that are keeping them awake at night.

The fundamental principles of CBT are drawn from cognitive

therapy, which has been used for many years to successfully treat depression, anxiety, panic attacks and other serious conditions including a range of phobias. CBT encourages the individual to focus on their current thoughts (or cognitive processes) and the behaviour that follows these thoughts. By modifying and rationalising thoughts, the individual will be able to tackle negative thinking and resolve knock-on effects (like insomnia).

Each perceived problem is broken down into manageable chunks which assess the individual's thoughts, emotions, feelings and actions in relation to that problem. Working through issues in a methodical way, and understanding how the constituent parts of a situation can be isolated – but also how they interrelate – can give a real insight into the impact of positive and negative thinking on your emotional state and on the decisions that you take as a consequence.

So why is CBT so useful for insomniacs? The University of Loughborough's Kevin Morgan explains: "People who can't sleep think about stuff. The dark bedroom is the best possible place to do some thinking, and eventually you're going to bump into an anxiety or a depressing thought, and CBT effectively teaches people ways to structure their thoughts, deal with them and discipline them. In the same way, other relaxation procedures can accelerate sleep onset, because they probably work through a cognitive mechanism.

"If you were to hold up CBT alongside hypnotic drugs and say what's the fundamental difference, you eat the drug and you do the therapy. CBT is developed from an understanding of where sleep goes wrong. Drugs are non-specific, they don't interact with some mechanism, they just render you dopey. CBT comes out of a research tradition that looks at how sleep works."

Kevin Morgan and his team at the Sleep Research Centre have used CBT in treating insomnia, and the results, as he explains, speak for themselves: "The world's summarised evidence on the subject of CBT for insomnia demonstrates that up to five hours of a CBT package of responses to insomnia can deliver long standing benefits to up to 80 per cent of all people with insomnia. Even the most sceptical person can see that in trial after trial, the components of CBT are proved to be effective in the management of chronic insomnia."

So if CBT would effectively provide long term management of insomnia in four out of every five sufferers, what prevents it becoming the standard treatment for the condition? Yes, you guessed it – money. But that's not the whole story, as Kevin Morgan adds: "There are a couple of issues, one is ownership within the UK healthcare system. You need a specialty within medicine that feels it owns insomnia, it needs a champion. If you look at the budgets invested in drugs [drug companies spend £1.5+ billion marketing their products per year in the UK alone] and you compare it to the kind of push behind talking therapies, then you realise there's a huge discrepancy. But that's simply the way the political economy works in healthcare delivery. If you've got a financially muscular champion like the pharmaceutical companies, that's powerful, whereas no shareholders are going to profit from the universal deployment of CBT."

But just because no-one's applying huge marketing budgets to the promotion of CBT and other talking therapies doesn't mean your right to these treatments is diminished. You're just going to have to fight harder, shout louder and wait longer to get access to what you want. Kevin Morgan adds: "These are psychological treatments, and everybody in this country has access to clinical psychology services on the NHS, but there are long waiting lists and the skills needed are expensive. It's very difficult to capture this stuff and put it in a bottle, so the challenge is, how can we take CBT messages and deliver them more widely and more cost effectively? The ultimate arbiter is does this treatment work, is it cost effective and will it compete successfully with alternative ways of treating the same thing?"

The answer seems to be overwhelmingly in the positive. And fortunately, the future is also starting to look brighter. Kevin Morgan adds: "Patients want CBT, the clinicians would rather not be prescribing drugs. Things are changing and I would be surprised if in five or ten years time things look like they do now. The nut to crack now is how to penetrate primary care and how to package and deliver these therapies."

Such is the popularity and effectiveness of CBT that a range of self-help products have already been developed to enable individuals to sample the basic theories behind the therapy for themselves. While CBT may be best delivered through a tailored programme of sessions with a qualified therapist, there is at least some sense in reading about the fundamental principles of the treatment if you think it may be of use. You can find self-help CDs and online courses – see the links section at the back of this book for more information on CBT.

SLEEP DIARIES – COGNITIVE BEHAVIORAL THERAPY

ANNABEL: "I saw a cognitive behaviour therapist. I really could see what he was trying to achieve but it just wasn't right for me. He did however give me some relaxing and breathing techniques that could help. I found that they worked, especially if I was stressed at night. They didn't so much help me sleep but made it a lot easier to relax myself so I could be in a better place to fall asleep."

DEAN: "I was keen to try out CBT, but in honesty I was too cowardly to go to the doctor and ask for a referral. Instead I found out about an online trial of a CBT based self-help package. So I signed up for that, and I did the exercises it recommended – simple things that helped me understand my behaviour in terms of my thinking leading up to events. I realised that I had a very negative mindset about problems – particularly work problems, and this was spilling out into every decision I made. It was also making sleep pretty hard, because I was wrestling with the whys and wherefores of my mounting problems at work. The CBT techniques helped me work on my attitude as much as anything, turning negative thoughts around and making some pretty hard decisions easier to bear. I think if I ever went through a period like this again, I'd definitely try to get on a proper course of treatment."

Sleeping pills and talking therapies like CBT are the main alternatives available to the insomniac on the NHS. If you step into the world of private treatment, other options for the management of insomnia – such as homeopathy, acupuncture and herbal medicine – open up to you. These therapies make their own impressive claims, and we'll take a closer look at them below, but Kevin Morgan counsels against a like-for-like comparison.

He says: "It's hard to compare CBT as an evidence based scenario with complementary medicine, where the evidence is thin. I have an interest in improving life for people with insomnia, so I've reviewed this evidence, but it's just not there.

"For some reason we feel comfortable telling people with insomnia about treatment with an impoverished database showing its efficacy. It's marketed on the basis that it's natural or that it is related to a personal outlook on life that is more holistic. But what is most reliably going to treat people with a chronic problem? The playing field isn't level. I have colleagues who are exploring all kinds of avenues in alternative and complementary systems but at the moment the strongest and most predictably effective alternative to pharmacology is the psychological approach."

End of story? Well possibly, but alternative and complementary therapies are gaining ground in the race to be accepted as credible partners or alternatives to standard medicine. And although the vast majority of these treatments are only available as private treatments, there are moves to incorporate some of the more successful treatments into the NHS, such as those on offer at the Royal London Homeopathic Hospital, which patients can access by referral only.

Taking on board Kevin Morgan's assertion that the playing field is not level, and acknowledging the clearly defined need for more exacting testing and regulation of treatments in the alternative field, these treatments are nonetheless part of the overall suite of therapies on offer to those with sleep problems, so we must look closer at what they purport to offer the sleeper.

Acupuncturist Lisa Sherman can lay claim to understanding both sides of the 'conventional medicine versus alternative medicine' argument. After studying for a first degree in molecular biology and working in lab research, Lisa decided to follow up on a growing interest in qigong and yoga by taking a degree in acupuncture. She is currently in clinical practice at the

Hammersmith Hospital in West London and also works in an integrated health centre in Islington. She's on the editorial committee of 'The Acupuncturist', which is the newsletter of the British Acupuncture Council and acts as their science correspondent.

So why does Lisa think that certain areas of medicine and research still view alternative therapies with scepticism? She explains: "I understand this position well, coming from a Western scientific background myself, and my own 'inner sceptic' and 'inner believer' have had some very interesting debates. The models used to explain pathology in traditional Chinese medicine are very different to those that Western science uses, and are based on a philosophical worldview which is very alien to the modern Western mind. Western scientists like to believe that they have a monopoly on the truth and that their description of reality is the only one that is valid. Anything outside that can't be 'true'.

"Some Western scientists hear acupuncturists use terms like 'yin', 'yang' and 'qi' and write them off as 'new age' nonsense without taking time to look any deeper. If they did, they might understand that what these terms are actually trying to convey are sophisticated descriptions of complex interacting systems that describe the body in terms of synthesis (the big picture) rather than analysis (the fine detail)."

So could it be possible that the rigidity of our thinking and scientific reasoning is preventing us from seeing more obvious and wide reaching issues relating to our health? Lisa Sherman certainly thinks so: "Doctors often like to know how things could possibly work, in terms of their own medical paradigm, before believing that they can work at all. They need the observations to fit their theory. This is actually contrary to the scientific method where theory comes from observation. The ancient Chinese were masters of observation. For example, they knew that people's emotions could play a major role in determining their physical as well as mental health, centuries before Western science embraced this concept.

"However, more and more research is discovering how acupuncture works in western terms and so doctors are beginning to come round to the possibility that there may actually be something in it. Luckily acupuncture even works on sceptics! My initially somewhat incredulous doctor/scientist husband was convinced when I used acupuncture on him for his heartburn and it worked, where conventional medication had not."

This is an interesting debate, and it will rage for years, especially as neither side seems to recognise each other's terms of classification for 'successful' treatment. But what we need to know is what benefits alternative therapies offer to the sleeper beyond their ability to relax the body and calm the mind. The cases for three of the most common areas of alternative therapy are made below:

Straight to the point – acupuncture

Q: How do you get a good night's sleep?

A: Acupuncture. It solved a period of long term insomnia almost overnight.

Acupuncture is a holistic approach to treatment dating back more than 2,000 years to its origins in the Far East. It is based on the philosophical theory that our bodies have a motivating energy – known as qi – which is composed of opposite and equal qualities called yin and yang. When these become imbalanced, illness follows.

Treatment involves the insertion of around six to 10 fine needles at various locations on the body. Once the needles are inserted, the patient will rest on the couch with the needles in for 15 to 20 minutes, before they are removed. Acupuncture should only ever be performed by a qualified acupuncturist. Additional techniques such as tuina (a form of massage), cupping (suction cup massage) and moxibustion (warming of the skin with a burning herb), may be employed if they are appropriate to the person's condition. Some practitioners are also qualified to prescribe Chinese herbs that are said to work synergistically with the acupuncture treatment.

So what should a patient expect from a session of acupuncture? Lisa Sherman explains: "The initial consultation for traditional acupuncture is typically one to one and a half hours long and involves taking a detailed case history. The practitioner will ask many wide ranging questions, not just about the person's insomnia, but also about many other aspects of their health and lifestyle. This broad picture of the whole person in the context of their environment helps the acupuncturist choose the appropriate treatment plan for that individual. There is usually time for a treatment at the end of the first session. The therapist will also recommend any appropriate lifestyle changes and may demonstrate breathing techniques or qigong exercises that will help the patient to relax and deal with stress. They will discuss the treatment plan and the likely progress of the course of therapy and give the patient the opportunity to ask any questions they may have.

"Follow-up sessions are shorter, typically 45 minutes to an hour, with a shorter initial consultation and a longer treatment. The patient typically feels very relaxed during the treatment and may even drop off to sleep on the table. Patients also usually report a good night's sleep on the day of the treatment. The initial benefit of the treatment typically lasts a few days and then begins to tail off, hence weekly treatments are recommended. As the person's body begins to rebalance itself, the positive effect of the treatment is extended over longer and longer periods of time, such that treatments can be more widely spaced out and eventually stopped altogether."

So what is it about acupuncture that makes this a suitable treatment for people with chronic sleep problems? Lisa Sherman adds: "Insomnia isn't a single disease entity, but a symptom with many possible underlying causes. The diagnostic methods used in traditional Chinese acupuncture try to discern the root cause of a person's sleeplessness and treat this accordingly. The acupuncture treatment will therefore be specifically tailored to the individual. Often people with insomnia are stuck in a negative psychological and physiological feedback cycle of anxiety-insomnia-tiredness-more anxiety. Acupuncture helps break this cycle and re-achieve balance by encouraging the process of homeostasis – the natural tendency of the body to find equilibrium.

"Acupuncture has been successfully used to treat sleep problems for centuries and is widely reported by today's patients to be very helpful in relieving insomnia. The scientific research carried out so far supports this anecdotal evidence, with some reports suggesting that it may have a nearly 90 per cent success rate for the treatment of insomnia. The speed at which the treatment works depends on the underlying cause of the insomnia. Some cases resolve very quickly, within two or three treatments, but others may require a course of six or 10 sessions for the problem to be resolved."

Given her scientific background, it's not surprising that Lisa Sherman is keen to accentuate the fact that its benefits can be demonstrated in terms of Western thinking, as well as in its traditional context. She explains: "Scientists are beginning to work out the mechanisms by which the needling of acupuncture points can have such a powerful effect, from a Western medical viewpoint. Needling has specific, well documented effects on the body, particularly on the nervous and endocrine systems. It influences the production of the body's communication substances – hormones and neurotransmitters. Through a complex series of signals to the body, acupuncture increases the production of calming neurochemicals such as serotonin, to promote relaxation and sleep. It stimulates the parasympathetic nervous system, which counteracts the stress induced 'fight or flight response' of the sympathetic nervous system, resulting in the 'relaxation response'."

One fairly obvious response from the first timer to acupuncture would be 'ouch, isn't that painful?', but Lisa Sherman is quick to reassure potential patients that the treatment is a very gentle form of therapy. She explains: "Acupuncture is very well tolerated by the vast majority of people and is remarkable for being almost completely side effect free, because its main function is to regulate the internal processes of the body and stimulate its own natural healing responses. There are few documented adverse reactions to acupuncture. In the hands of properly trained, qualified acupuncturists, the technique is very safe. One landmark study published in the British Medical Journal reported that no serious adverse events had occurred during the 34,000 acupuncture treatments surveyed."

According to Lisa Sherman, acupuncture is also safe as a complementary therapy. "It can be used alongside Western allopathic interventions," she says. "Often, as the acupuncture begins to take effect, the need for pharmacological therapy decreases, however any reduction in medication should be done in consultation with the patient's GP."

But for all its reported power, acupuncture still works best as part of a programme of lifestyle changes such as those outlined in part three. This is the cornerstone of holistic therapies in general – suggesting that the patient must be ready to treat the lifestyle imbalance and not just rely on the therapy to do the job for them.

Lisa Sherman adds: "The cause of insomnia is often rooted in an individual's lifestyle choices and may be related to diet, exercise and emotional health. Acupuncturists seek to discern, through extensive questioning, an accurate picture of the person in the context of their life and in addition to using needling and other therapeutic techniques, they will often advise patients of ways that they can modify their behaviour to improve their health. People who are willing to recognise the impact of their lifestyle choices on their health are more likely to be able to change any circumstances that are contributing to the problem. These changes can often have a dramatic and rapid beneficial effect. Often, it seems, the more serious the imbalance, the more dramatic the effect of the treatment."

Though it must be stressed once again that acupuncture is only to be carried out by a qualified acupuncturist, it is possible to use elements of the theory yourself in a different therapy known as acupressure. The following are some acupressure points that may help with the relief of sleep problems, as advised by Lisa Sherman. In each case, press and hold these points with thumb or fingertip, for about three minutes each, while keeping the eyes closed and taking long, slow, deep, comfortable abdominal breaths:

Heart 7. With the palm of the hand facing you, this point is located on the wrist crease, in line with the little finger.

Pericardium 6. Located in the middle of the inner side of the forearm (between the two tendons), three finger widths from the wrist crease.

Ren 17. This point lies in an indentation on the centre of the breastbone, about four finger widths up from the base of the bone, approximately in line with the nipples.

Bladder 62. Located in the first hollow directly below the outer anklebone.

Yintang. This point is in the centre of the forehead, between the eyebrows.

SLEEP DIARY – ACUPUNCTURE

GLORIA: "The menopause hit me like an out of control truck. As if all the other symptoms weren't enough to cope with I was also having massive hot flushes. These engulfed me by day and by night, causing me great distress and endless hours of discomfort and lost sleep.

"For many reasons I didn't want to take the HRT route so I consulted an

acupuncturist. I told her that being deprived of sleep was the worst aspect of all, so she concentrated on eradicating the damp from my body to reduce the flushes and so make my nights more bearable. She advised me on diet, too, to help with the dampness. At first I saw her every week for six weeks, then every month.

"It worked, gradually, and after four months the night sweats were much reduced and I was only waking about three times in the night as opposed to 10 or 12 times. I've been having acupuncture for a year now and am happy to say that, while the flushes still come and go, they have been minimised to the extent that I hardly notice them. And I sleep like a top!"

Like with like – homeopathy

The Society of Homeopaths describes homeopathy as follows: "It is a gentle, holistic system of healing, suitable for everyone, young and old. Homeopathy focuses on you as an individual, concentrating on treating your specific physical and emotional symptoms, to give long lasting benefits. The therapy is based on the theory of treating 'like with like'. Homeopathic remedies are highly diluted natural substances that, if given in stronger doses to a healthy person, would produce the symptoms the medicine is prescribed for. In the assessment of you, the patient, homeopaths will take into account the range of physical, emotional and lifestyle factors in order to prescribe the right medicine(s)."

Homeopathic medicines are drawn from the plant, mineral and animal worlds. A regulated homeopathic pharmacy prepares the medicines by blending raw extracts with alcohol to create a tincture which is then further diluted with water to create varying potencies of medicine, often indicated in over the counter treatments as 6c or 30c potencies. Homeopathy is used for a wide range of treatments – from eczema to fever, from mild depression to chronic fatigue.

Andrew Kirk has been working in homeopathy since 1993 – he's now the chairman of leading industry body The Society of Homeopaths. He believes the emphasis on the holistic approach is the key to understanding why homeopathy offers such a radical alternative to standard medicine. He says: "In 'normal' medicine, generally speaking, there's a dualistic split between mind and body – doctors take care of the body and psychologists take care of the mind. In homeopathy, you're just dealing with energy and energy manifests itself as a disturbance on any level. The issue may not be important or it may be the trigger. If somebody has what homeopaths in the 18th century called 'the vital force' then that disturbance manifests itself in all levels. So we look at the whole picture. We need to know what's going on psychologically, but that isn't the focus of what we're treating. We treat everything with equal weight."

The hardest thing to understand about homeopathy for people coming from a background of traditional medical treatments, is the apparent lack of labels for disease – we are familiar with specific conditions receiving specific treatments, but as Andrew Kirk argues, this isn't necessarily the most appropriate response. He adds: "Homeopaths are not focused on disease, we're focused on wellness. The problem with medicine is that it stops at a certain level of primary cause, and then they'll discover something deeper and stop there. From our point of view things happen on a level that we can't perceive. Homeopathy is much more related to a physics explanation of how energy works rather than a material explanation of how chemistry works. All disease labels are arbitrary. It's got more to do with an individual's family history and susceptibility. If you treat insomnia as a chronic disease entity, that would just be a useful peg to hang things on but it wouldn't necessarily tell you anything."

Susceptibility is a key word for homeopaths, particularly in the treatment of sleep problems. Andrew Kirk explains: "There are people who for various historical reasons have susceptibility in the area of sleep and that's their trigger whenever anything goes wrong. With other people there might be a particular episode like a sick relative being nursed through the night, so the sleep pattern is affected by this particular circumstance and that becomes the problem. It's the same thing with babies waking every hour. The event itself could be nothing to do with sleep, but sleep is the susceptibility."

Andrew Kirk's idea that a proportion of the population has a susceptibility to sleep problems echoes the view of Kevin Morgan, expressed way back in part one, that up to a third of us has a capacity for insomnia which circumstance brings to the fore.

The first step in homeopathic treatment, like that in acupuncture and other holistic treatments, is the consultation. It is during this hour or so of general discussion that Andrew Kirk and his colleagues 'draw out' the essential facts of their patient's condition. He explains: "Generally a patient will pretty much tell you everything you need to know. It may be that they came to talk about sleep, but then they go on to talk about relationship problems or something else. Quite often events that are more recent are echoes of something from years before. If say, a patient's mother died when they were 25, that might be what they've come in with, but the root issue is that their father died when they were 11, and that's what you treat. There are more than

3,000 remedies in homeopathy and every single one is a sleep remedy. We look at what's unusual about the particular case, because that's about the individual, and that's the way we treat patients – as individuals."

While he is anxious to stress that homeopathy has a place as a complementary therapy alongside traditional medicine, Andrew Kirk is aware of the differences in the disciplines: "There's an industrial approach to treating large numbers of people that the NHS has to adopt. It doesn't work for homeopathic medicine."

Medication in the form of sleeping pills is a particular obstacle faced by homeopaths, and Andrew Kirk is predictably and understandably scornful of their long term application. He adds: "The problem with any medication comes when it is prescribed for any length of time without anyone bothering to find out what the problem is. I tend to see people who tranquilisers don't tranquilise and sleeping tablets don't make sleep – they keep them awake in fact."

There is an understandable reluctance among patients to give up their medications, even if they have stopped working effectively. As Andrew Kirk explains, the ultimate choice has to remain with the patient. He explains: "If the medication was completely masking the symptoms but wasn't essential to maintain life, I'd say you have to make a choice, there's no point in me treating you if I can't see whether the remedy is working. But in an ideal world it is better that people wean themselves off any medication slowly."

One of the primary concerns that people have when going private is the duration and cost of treatment, but as Andrew Kirk explains, in homeopathy neither is necessarily an issue:

"Self-help treatments are available over the counter. If somebody rings me and says 'can you do something to help me sleep?' then I'd say go to the chemist and try [the homeopathic treatment] Coffea, and then if that first line of defence doesn't work come to me and we'll delve deeper. But if the over the counter remedy works that's great. When people do come to me, if there's a distinctive enough picture I can prescribe a remedy that will work rapidly. In fact, the benefit can be immediate in most cases. When you come to a homeopath you are looking at a course of treatment, but things should improve within a week to 10 days."

The vast majority of homeopathic remedies are available through a qualified practitioner only, but many shops are now stocking ranges of remedies, and some of these can be used for sleep problems. Here's Andrew Kirk's selection from some of the more readily available remedies:

Aconite is a remedy for anyone who experiences sudden starts out of sleep, aconite is also used for restlessness and a general feeling of unease. It is commonly used for elderly people living alone and prone to anxiety.

Arnica is a common remedy for any form of physical overexertion. It aims to counter the sleep disturbance caused by aching muscles.

Arsen Alb is a treatment for anxiety attacks, which seem to occur around midnight. It is used to treat people who feel such anxiety that they are forced out of bed and have to pace the floor.

Avena Sativa aims to ease longer term nervous exhaustion. The worry itself might be over, but the sleeping problem persists. This is commonly used for people who have been ill for a long period and who have developed an irregular sleeping pattern.

Belladonna is used specifically as a fever remedy. If the patient is suffering from hallucinations, restlessness and severe anxiety that may even manifest itself through screaming or talking in sleep, then this treatment is often advised.

Coffea, as the name suggests, is a treatment for overstimulation. This may come from ingesting too many stimulants, like coffee, but it may also be due to positive stimulation – for example, nervous excitement about an event like Christmas.

Nux Vomica is a 'workaholic' remedy, used to treat people who are addicted to stimulants. These are people whose nervous systems are washed out by overwork, so they take stimulants – alcohol, nicotine, caffeine etc. – to keep themselves going. When they work too hard, this becomes a chronic state and may lead to sleeplessness. It's also a hangover cure. In addition, Nux Vomica is used for so-called 'nightwatching' – when people have become familiar with sitting awake for long periods of the night, perhaps nursing a sick relative.

Phosphorus is used for people with milder anxieties – commonly fear of ghosts, monsters and the dark. Once again it is commonly used for the elderly, but also for children.

Rhus Tox is another remedy for physical exertion, particularly when it is manifested as a desire to stretch out. It is also used as a remedy for restless leg syndrome as it is good for random twitches.

Finally, a couple of less common remedies, which may only be available in some outlets: **opium** is used for sleeplessness after serious trauma or even terror and **stramonium** is used to treat extreme night terrors in children, and the rare occurrence of sleeping with the eyes open.

Please remember that it is essential to follow the issuer's guidance with any remedies and medicines, whether purchased over the counter or prescribed.

SLEEP DIARY – HOMEOPATHY

GLORIA: *"My sleep pattern went awry after I'd been looking after my mother through her final illness. I would fall asleep but then wake up after an hour or so and not be able to get back to sleep again for ages. I consulted the homeopath who had treated me successfully in the past for migraines.*

"He asked me about three or four dozen questions to build up a picture of my physical and emotional condition as well as my way of life. It's always strange to be asked 'What makes you angry' or 'When did you last cry' in a situation like this.

"He gave me some little sulphur tablets to take, like ants' eggs. They dissolve under your tongue. The idea was to restore my balance and get me back on track and into a better routine. Very soon my sleeping improved, probably within two or three days. I continued seeing the homeopath once a month for another six months or so and my sleep pattern has remained very good. I am really glad I tackled the problem and I think this was the best way to do it. I've since recommended a friend to do the same."

Nature's way? – herbal remedies

Herbal remedies for sleepers are intended to relax and calm the user, paving the way for a better night's rest. While there's not a specific herbal 'cure' for sleeplessness, a number of herbs do seem to have a sedative effect on some people.

The attraction of herbal remedies – both the remedies available from professional herbalists and the over the counter remedies that can be found in health food shops and chemists – is that they lack the powerful, negative side effects prevalent in pharmaceutical remedies. While it's true that herbal remedies seem less likely to cause side effects, there is insufficient research available to be certain that there are no possible long term effects, or indeed whether the remedies themselves have any significant long term benefit to the user.

The most common herbs used to induce sleep are valerian, hops and chamomile. These can be taken orally as teas and tinctures. They are often found in combination as the ingredients of herbal sleeping tablets. Other herbal remedies may aid restful sleep by acting as pain relievers – St John's Wort is the best known of these and may be helpful for people with aching joints or muscles.

Herbal medicine is a very subjective area. The cynical view is that the treatments work by positive association – because we are told that they are 'natural' then we assume they must do us good and we feel better as a consequence – the so-called placebo effect. On the other hand these are treatments that have been in use for centuries and many people claim they have derived great benefit from them. It is a matter best left to the individual – but if you plan to sample herbal remedies consult a professional herbalist and, if you are on any prescription medication, speak to your doctor about potential clashes between treatments.

A further advantage of consulting a herbalist rather than purchasing a ready made remedy is that herbalists share the philosophy of holistic treatment that is common in many alternative therapies. Through consultation and discussion of your specific circumstances, they may prescribe a remedy that is markedly different from that given to someone else presenting the same symptoms.

Bear in mind also that although these remedies do claim to be natural, they are still sedatives, and consequently, they may be masking a problem rather than addressing it – and they certainly should not be used on a nightly basis.

SLEEP DIARIES – HERBAL REMEDIES

EMILY: "*After I'd been through an awful period without sleep a friend persuaded me to take herbal sleeping tablets. I persevered with them for a couple of weeks but they didn't work at all for me. Firstly, I'd convinced myself that they weren't going to work, so they didn't really stand a chance, and secondly I just wasn't comfortable with the idea of taking any pills.*"

FRANCES: "*I purchased some from the chemists and health food shops. I've tried a variety, with varying results. There's a tincture of valerian and hops which I drank diluted in water before going to bed. It did seem to have an effect but I got a bit fed up with it as it tasted so revolting. I now take herbal sleeping tablets, but only occasionally as I'm trying not to rely on anything like that any more.*"

However you view alternative therapies, they are playing a larger role in healthcare than ever before. This may be due in part to a general dissatisfaction with drug based medicine and its perceived trap of dependency, or it may be linked to a broader realisation that the fields of mental and physical health are inextricably linked. Certainly the common thread that binds all holistic treatments – the detailed consultation and the insistence on a general rebalancing of the patient's lifestyle to complement any therapy given – is an encouraging way to view treatment of stress-related illness.

But for all this, the official line remains constant – the evidence supporting the effectiveness of alternative therapies in the treatment of chronic conditions like insomnia is thin. So do they work? It seems an odd thing to say, given that some of these therapies date back thousands of years, but perhaps only time will tell.

KEY POINTS

Patient choice. Insomnia treatments available on the NHS fall into two camps – pharmaceutical treatments and psychiatric treatments.

The drugs question. Sleeping pills can offer short term benefits to the chronically sleep deprived or to those seeking to redress their sleep pattern. But they are a short term solution only, and just mask the underlying problem.

Talk about it. Talking therapies such as Cognitive Behavioural Therapy (CBT) have been proved to be successful in treating the majority of insomniacs, but they are costly and not readily available. But this trend is changing, and as the evidence becomes more overwhelmingly favourable, CBT is set to become the most effective mainstream treatment for insomnia.

Another way. Alternative therapies are becoming increasingly popular, and though most are only available privately, some are becoming incorporated into NHS specialist hospitals. Although the evidence for the effectiveness of these treatments is not as rigorous as that for mainstream treatments, many people report significant benefits from treatments such as acupuncture, homeopathy and herbal medicine. More research is needed to establish the true level of benefit offered by these treatments, but their holistic approach encourages the insomniac to consider a range of lifestyle changes which is beneficial to sleep and to health in general.

PART FIVE: When sleep fails – common sleep disorders

There is an outside chance that once you've addressed all the issues of environment, routine and mental well-being detailed above, you are still left with a poor sleep pattern or a feeling of acute exhaustion in the day. This might be because you simply haven't found the right remedy, or it might be because you have an underlying sleep disorder that requires specific treatment.

As we discussed back in part one, there's a huge list of sleep disorders. We can only scratch the surface of sleep disorders here, but we'll take a look at some of the more common disorders and highlight possible areas of treatment or management. We'll be looking at the following:

★ snoring and obstructive sleep apnoea

★ circadian rhythm disorders – including jet lag and shift work

★ restless leg syndrome

★ nightmares and night terrors

★ sleepwalking

★ narcolepsy

No laughing matter – snoring and obstructive sleep apnoea

Snoring is often regarded as a bit of a 'joke' complaint. Snorers are typically cast as overweight slobs or heavy drinkers who don't have the social awareness to realise their night time noises are driving their partners mad. Most of all, snoring is regarded as a mild irritation rather than a serious complaint. There's a tiny grain of truth hidden in all this prejudice – weight and alcohol consumption do play a part in snoring, but the full story of snoring and the serious condition known as obstructive sleep apnoea, which is often incorrectly bracketed as snoring, is much less of a joke.

The British Snoring and Sleep Apnoea Association has spent the best part of two decades fighting prejudice about these conditions, while aiming to spread information and guidance about treatments – because snoring and sleep apnoea are both treatable, if not curable, conditions. They've kindly provided the following advice to help suffers and their long suffering partners cope with the impact of these conditions.

Let's start with snoring. This is a more common condition than you might realise – more than 40 per cent of the UK population snores (and presumably up to another 40 per cent lies there listening to them). Snoring is defined as a coarse sound made by vibrations of the soft palate and other tissue in the mouth, nose and throat. This is caused by turbulence from a blockage in the airway. Weight and booze aren't the only triggers for a night of snores – other potential causes of the complaint include smoking, allergies, sleeping position, nasal stuffiness and small or collapsed nostrils. If you are used to breathing through your mouth in the daytime, you're also more likely to snore at night. Snoring may be attributed to any of these causes individually, or to a whole range of them.

With such a variety of causes around, it's vital to identify what sort of snorer you are if you want to get the right treatment. The British Snoring and Sleep Apnoea Association has developed a series of self-tests which allow snorers to narrow the field of possible causes. The first test involves closing one nostril and trying to breathe through the other – if that nostril collapses, or if you find that you need to prop the nostril open to breathe easily then you may benefit from nasal dilators or nasal strips, which work to gently keep the airway clear.

Test two involves opening your mouth and making a snoring sound. Then try the same sound with your mouth closed. If you can only snore with your mouth open, you're a mouth breather, and you should try a product known as 'chin-up strips', which keeps the mouth closed while you sleep.

In the final test, stick your tongue out as far as it will go and grip it between your teeth, then try to make a snoring noise. If the noise is reduced with your tongue in a forward position, you are what is known as a 'tongue base snorer' and the scary sounding mandibular advancement device – a remedy that brings your jaw and tongue forward – is your best option.

What else can you do to reduce the risk of snoring? Obviously it's a good idea to keep your weight down and cut back on alcohol and other stimulants – make sure you stop drinking at least four hours prior to bedtime. Your sleeping position can also be a factor – avoid sleeping on your back if possible. Some people even swear by the old remedy of a tennis ball tied to the back to stop themselves inadvertently rolling over in the night.

If you've eliminated all of the above possibilities and tried all the available remedies and you're still snoring then you might consider corrective surgery, though this is recommended only as a last resort.

The other possibility is that your snoring is caused by obstructive sleep apnoea, a more serious, though related, condition that leaves sufferers literally gasping for breath at night and excessively sleepy during the day.

Sleep apnoea is pretty common as far as sleep disorders go – affecting around four per cent of men and two per cent of women in the UK. The condition occurs when the sleeper's breathing is stopped by an obstruction in the back of the throat. Breathing may be blocked for anything between 10 and 20 seconds, at which time the brain wakes the sleeper, usually with a loud snore or snort. This may happen several times in the night, resulting in severely disturbed sleep, though it is possible for the sufferer to wake the next morning unaware of the true fragmented nature of their night's sleep.

While sleep apnoea and snoring share some causes – especially excessive alcohol consumption and weight – the symptoms of sleep apnoea are often much more extreme and persistent. In addition to sleepiness and heavy snoring, sufferers may show signs of anxiety or depression, forgetfulness and irritability. Sleep apnoea is one of the chief causes of chronic daytime fatigue, and consequently it makes its sufferers liable to all the associated risks, including dangerous driving, incapacity while operating machinery and an inability to carry out essential tasks safely.

Sleep apnoea can only be diagnosed by an intense study of your sleep pattern and assessment of the amount of oxygen your body is getting during sleep. This will normally follow a referral by your GP (who should be your immediate port of call if you suspect you have obstructive sleep apnoea) and will involve a night in hospital being monitored. The results of this test will help to determine the severity of your condition and the most appropriate treatment.

Swiss sleep researchers have discovered that exercising the airways by playing a wind instrument, such as the traditional aboriginal didgeridoo, can play a part in helping people with mild sleep apnoea. Apparently, singing regularly may have a similar effect.

In mild cases, sleep apnoea can be treated in much the same way as snoring – with simple adjustments to diet, lifestyle and sleeping position. In moderate cases, the mandibular advancement device mentioned above may be effective. For more severe sleep apnoea, a treatment known as CPAP (continuous positive airways pressure) has achieved good results in reducing symptoms. CPAP uses a device which automatically controls the pressure in the sleeper's airways via a mask. They look cumbersome, but there's a wide range available and some are very small and discreet. If your condition has been diagnosed by a hospital specialist, you will probably be prescribed one of these devices to treat your apnoea.

In addition to obstructive sleep apnoea, there is also a condition called central sleep apnoea, which has the same consequence – i.e. breaks in breathing while sleeping – but is actually connected to faulty brain signals rather than a physical obstruction. Consequently treatment is more complex and tends to be focused very much on individual needs. A third condition, known as mixed sleep apnoea, is a combination of the other two conditions.

Circadian rhythm disorders

Our internal body clock, the circadian rhythm, is what keeps our sleep pattern regular. It's mainly instinctive, but it can also be trained by the good discipline of going to bed and getting up at regular times. Some people have a faulty circadian rhythm, which results in the fragmenting of their usual sleep pattern. This fault may be due to a sudden change in routine, or to a generally disorganised sleep routine. It may also be linked to a more serious condition like Alzheimer's disease.

In most cases, circadian rhythm disorders are transient – i.e. they are linked to a temporary break in an established routine. These include jet lag, shift work, and the consequences of an illness that has caused the sufferer to sleep at irregular times during the day. These transient disorders may well resolve themselves in time when the body has readjusted to the new routine, or has overcome the shock of a switch in time zones (usually around the time you're packing to come home from your holiday). But it is possible for these transient disorders to escalate into more chronic conditions, particularly if other factors are also present – like stress at work or increased alcohol consumption.

Chronic circadian rhythm disorders are divided into three areas – delayed sleep-phase syndrome (DSPS), advanced sleep-phase syndrome (ASPS) and irregular sleep-wake cycle (ISWC). With DSPS, sleepers find it hard to get to sleep and often lie-in for long periods – hence the reason it is often mistaken for 'laziness' in teenagers. ASPS is the reverse, where people go to bed early and wake before dawn and ISWC has absolutely no set pattern of waking and sleeping. Sufferers of any of these conditions may ultimately sleep as long as a normal sleeper, but the antisocial consequences of an abnormal sleep pattern are normally enough to encourage sufferers to seek treatment.

Effective control of circadian rhythm disorders is possible, and treatment varies according to severity. Treatment for the chronic disorders usually takes the form of a version of behavioural therapy designed to address the underlying reasons for the shift in sleep pattern, using environmental and psychological tools to help the sleeper gradually readjust their sleep pattern along more traditional lines. Pharmaceutical treatments are available that attempt a similar shift, but as with all drugs these may have certain undesirable side effects.

There's a wider variety of treatments available for the transient disorders, ranging from drugs to alternative therapies to old wives' tales. Jet lag, the most common transient disorder, is caused by a combination of factors – principally crossing time zones, but also physical condition, the dry atmosphere and stale air of the aircraft, alcohol and caffeine and lack of exercise. While most people think of jet lag as an unavoidable downside of long haul flights, it can also be a contributing factor in other travellers' maladies. A World Health Organisation report links the debilitating effects of jet lag with diarrhoea, affecting about 50 per cent of long haul travellers.

A 'cure' for jet lag would be a holy grail for the frequent traveller, and no product has yet managed this bold claim, though plenty are trying. Miers Laboratories, based in New Zealand, has created a homeopathic treatment called No-Jet-Lag which has enjoyed some success on trial with air cabin crews. To complement this remedy, they have developed a checklist of essential tips for reducing and managing jet lag.

These include relaxing pre-flight, and trying to get good rest on the night before. If you're going on holiday that means being a bit more organised when planning and packing – people who leave it to the last minute create stress and that has an impact on the journey. It's also important to keep hydrated with plenty of water (not alcohol or caffeine) on the flight and to use some sleep aids (such as blindfold, earplugs and neck pillow) to ensure you sleep well on a long haul flight and don't throw your routine out too drastically. Exercising on the flight also helps to counter the effects of jet lag – as well as decreasing the likelihood of blood clots.

Everyone's got a pet 'cure' for jet lag. Some people claim that flying westwards causes less jet lag than flying east, and that daytime flights are better for avoiding jet lag than night flights. Of course, the ultimate cure is to stay at home, but where's the fun in that?

Readjusting yourself gently to a new sleeping pattern is the key for shift workers who suffer from transient circadian rhythm disorder. It's possible to persuade your brain that it's time for sleep by following the kind of strict sleep routine described in parts two and three – if you're working nights, you'll need to convince your brain that 8am is bedtime, which means using blackout curtains, earplugs, eye mask and all of the other paraphernalia of bedtime, including warm baths, relaxation techniques and gentle winding down exercises like yoga or meditation and a cool room without distractions. The hardest part is keeping the noise of the outside world at bay, but if you can switch off effectively, there's every reason to expect your body and mind to adapt to a major change in sleep routine quickly and effectively.

Restless leg syndrome

As the name suggests, restless leg syndrome (RLS) causes discomfort to the extent that sufferers often feel compelled to get out of bed and pace around the room until the feeling eases. Understandably this can cause considerable disruption to the sleep pattern. A variant of RLS is called periodic limb movement, which presents itself as a jerkiness affecting a particular limb, causing broken sleep. This condition occurs most commonly in light, non-REM sleep.

The exact cause of RLS is not known, but it does seem to be more prevalent in older people and in women, especially those undergoing hormonal changes (for example during pregnancy) as well as those suffering from iron deficiency, anaemia or anyone who gives blood frequently. Some experts believe the condition may be linked to diabetes, though this connection is not well established.

Lifestyle changes can help to relieve the severity of RLS – especially reducing stimulants like caffeine and alcohol before bed. Since there appear to be links to diet and certain vitamin and mineral deficiencies, food and food supplements can play a major part – make sure you eat a balanced diet with plenty of fruit and vegetables and supplement this with iron and vitamin B12 if necessary. Other treatments that work for some people include drinking a glass of milk before bed and keeping the affected limb cool – either by keeping the covers off it, or by pressing a cool towel to the affected limb, or showering before bed. Acupressure, massage and stretching exercises have been found to be of some benefit in many cases. In more serious cases the symptoms of RLS can be eased with prescription medication like the Parkinson's disease drug L-Dopa, which can help to reduce tremors in the legs.

Nightmares and night terrors

Nightmares are common throughout life – the British Association for Counselling and Psychotherapy reports that as many as one in 10 adults regularly experience nightmares. These can cause sleep disturbance, especially if a nightmare is sufficiently vivid to wake the sleeper and cause disorientation and fear. Nightmares become less frequent with age.

A more extreme variant of this phenomenon, known as night terrors, mainly occurs in pre-teen children. There's no definitive explanation for this disorder, which may result in what appears to be a state of extreme distress – screaming, crying and apparent wakefulness – but is actually a part of sleep which a child may not even remember the next day.

It's hard for parents to stand by and watch this trauma unfold, so rest assured that you won't be doing any harm if you do decide to wake and gently reassure your child. Turning the light on or taking the child into another room may be sufficient to break the terror and wake the child. While your child is waking, it is vital to calmly reassure them that all is well, as this will also help them relax back into sleep.

There's no specific cure for this condition – it may be linked to psychological factors like excessive stress, or to being overtired, or it may even be part of a particular worry about home, school or relationships. Some people feel that temperature plays a part in night terrors and nightmares, as a cooler bedroom appears to lower the likelihood of these disturbances. It's normally a passing phase, though if it does continue for months rather than weeks, it's worth seeking medical or psychiatric advice to help you dig deeper into the underlying causes.

Sleepwalking

Sleepwalking is another condition that's common in children, though many adults also sleepwalk. As with night terrors, it's rare for the sleepwalker to remember their physical actions after the event. Many people believe that it's dangerous to wake a sleepwalker, but this isn't actually the case. If woken, a sleepwalker is likely to be extremely disorientated and upset, but it's better to wake them than to allow a potentially dangerous situation to occur – some sleepwalkers are capable of very complex actions such as opening doors and driving, and they may cause themselves or others harm if not checked.

If you're faced with a sleepwalker, try to get them safely back into bed, whether by waking them and gently reassuring them, or simply by guiding them while they sleep. The condition may be linked to a specific event or trauma, such as loss of a job, extreme terror or a bereavement, but it can be a symptom of a much milder disturbance. In any case, sleepwalking presents no danger to the sufferer in itself.

While there's no specific cure, it can be useful to tackle the root cause of the disturbance with hypnotherapy, or simply with a calm and relaxing pre-sleep routine. Sleepwalkers are advised to avoid alcohol and other stimulants and to avoid becoming excessively tired. In more extreme cases, it is possible to use certain antidepressant drugs to manage sleepwalking.

Narcolepsy

This is a neurological condition in which the brain's normal ability to switch between sleeping and waking is faulty. Sufferers may fall asleep suddenly during the day and will almost always experience a broken sleep pattern and excessive tiredness. This is also a condition without a comprehensive explanation. It appears that sticking to a rigid sleep routine can help to ease the effects of narcolepsy, while drugs are also commonly used in treatment. Sufferers may also be prone to another condition called cataplexy, in which an individual may suffer sudden and temporary muscular weakness – ranging from a drooping head to total collapse depending on the severity of the attack and the level of stress.

Digging deeper

There are many, many more sleep disorders, ranging from the transient to the chronic. Each of these is likely to lead to a serious sleep deficit, so it's always vital to seek medical advice if you are concerned about your sleep or you're constantly tired and lethargic in the daytime. Sleep disorders can rule your life, and one option is to seek treatment at one of the UK's specialist sleep centres – these are clinics focused solely on the diagnosis and treatment of sleep disorders.

The UK's largest sleep clinic is at Papworth Hospital in Cambridgeshire. It is an NHS run clinic, but patients can only access the clinic's range of services by referral from a GP. The sleep clinic at Papworth treats patients with a range of disorders and sleep difficulties – from obstructive sleep apnoea to sleep-walking and many others.

In addition to Papworth, there are many private sleep clinics in the UK – with two of the largest being the London Sleep Centre and the Edinburgh Sleep Centre. It is also possible to access treatment from these clinics by GP referral, though treatment is costly and not all primary care trusts will stump up the cash for referrals. If you have private healthcare insurance, you may be able to access treatments this way, or it might just be worth biting the bullet and paying out for specialist help. After all, if people are prepared to pay thousands of pounds for new breasts and higher buttocks, who could possibly put a price on a good night's sleep?

And finally...

For those lucky souls who find that going to sleep and staying asleep comes naturally, the mysteries of sleep might as well remain just that – a mystery. But for anyone who has ever suffered an episode of sleeplessness, however short it may have been, the fear of never getting a good night's sleep again is very real – and this makes it essential to grasp the processes and pitfalls of sleep routines and the advantages and disadvantages of the environmental changes, treatments and therapies available to the sleep deprived. This book has given you an essential tool kit of thoughts and suggestions that will help you approach any episode of sleeplessness in the future with more confidence and direction.

Whether this book has pointed you towards a specific answer or just a whole load of new questions about your own sleep, it will have opened your eyes to the sheer vastness of sleep problems and remedies and helped you realise that no-one needs to endure their sleep problems in silence. If you're keen to delve deeper, you'll find a list of useful links at the end of this book. Happy hunting and sleep tight.

AFTERWORD: 'Guinea pigs' revisited

Way back in part one we first met the sleep 'guinea pigs' who agreed to let us share their efforts to improve their sleep. During their journeys they've tried and tested a wide range of treatments, therapies and lifestyle changes. Before we leave them to a hard earned rest, let's catch up with them one more time to get an idea of the progress they've made in their own search for a good night's rest:

Annabel feared that she'd never be able to get back into a normal sleep pattern. Despite trying a broad range of treatments and therapies, Annabel is still searching for a solution to her chronic sleep problems. Her main concern seems to be an in-built aversion to deep sleep – as she puts it herself, she's spent so long not sleeping that she's actually frightened of the idea of deep sleep. Though Annabel found cognitive behavioural therapy didn't help in her case, a talking therapy may be what she needs to get beyond the irrational fears of sleeping that she's currently experiencing.

Barbara was looking for a remedy that would allow her to relax fully into sleep and go through the night without waking periods. She's also struggled to find a remedy that meets her needs –

though she's at the opposite end of the chronicity scale to Annabel. However, she has found some positive benefit from relaxation and breathing techniques, and she hopes to incorporate these into her sleep routine. At Barbara's age, fragmented sleep is common, so the chances of finding a long term fix for nocturnal waking are slim, but at the very least she should be able to minimise her waking periods with these newly acquired deep breathing and relaxing exercises.

Carole was keen to find a solution that allowed her to escape from her busy daily routine and relax into sleep. By radically redesigning the space in which she sleeps and developing a personal relaxation strategy, Carole has achieved her goal and now feels the quality and reliability of her sleep is markedly improved. To help her relax still further, she intends to find out more about massage and reflexology.

Dean was looking for a way to relax himself back into sleep if he woke during the night. His major environmental change involved buying a new bed that brought a huge improvement to the effectiveness of his mattress and provided a much more comfortable rest. His specific concern regarding the long waking periods he experienced on a regular basis was addressed by studying the key principles of cognitive behavioural therapy and adapting these to his own routine of relaxation and problem solving. His stress levels have dropped significantly, and a combination of better sleep and more effective thinking has helped him to develop a much more positive outlook on life.

Emily was prepared to try anything to correct the balance of her sleep, as she feared it was intruding on her family life and her general well-being. She was one of the most prolific guinea pigs, trying light and sound pollution techniques, aromatherapy, herbal medicines and hypnotherapy. It was this final treatment which worked for Emily, and she now sleeps better than at any time in her adult life. Underlying issues regarding some of the traumatic events that contributed to such a fragmented sleep pattern are still unresolved, but Emily is committed to exploring talking therapies.

Frances wanted to regulate her sleep pattern and ensure that outside disturbance didn't intrude too much on her nights. Basic environmental changes like eye masks and earplugs worked for her in the short term, but the inconvenience and discomfort of these solutions ultimately outweighed their benefits. Her sleep pattern has improved, due in part to a combination of various improvements to her sleep routine, but also due to a more stable period at work and home, lowering stress levels and allowing her to concentrate on relaxing into sleep.

Gloria was keen to avoid conventional medicine for her sleep problems. She tried acupuncture and homeopathic treatments and reported success with both – and although the acupuncture in particular was a slow process, she feels confident that the holistic approach of these treatments has benefited her overall sleep pattern.

Useful links and further information

This is a list of some of the resources that have been useful in the writing of this book – it's not an exhaustive list of sleep-related information – there's plenty more out there, but be warned that many internet sites offer 'general' information with a heavy bias towards the product or service they are trying to peddle, so use caution if you're following up any advice from these sites – and remember that information from a website is never an acceptable substitute for medical opinion.

Acupuncture: British Acupuncture Council, **www.acupuncture.org.uk**, 020 8735 0400

Arc Health, **www.arc-health.co.uk**, 020 7833 1688

Aromatherapy and reflexology: Aries aromatherapy and beauty clinic, **www.ariesbeauty.co.uk**, 01745 561310

Beds and mattresses: The Sleep Council, **www.sleepcouncil.com**, 0845 058 4595

Cognitive Behavioural Therapy: British Association for Behavioural and Cognitive Psychotherapies (BABCP), **www.babcp.com**, 01254 875277

Earplugs: Snorestore (retail outlet), **www.snorestore.co.uk**, 020 8861 3149

EMFs and microwaves: Powerwatch, **www.powerwatch.org.uk**

Feng Shui: The Feng Shui Academy/Robert Gray, **www.feng-shuiacademy.co.uk**, 0871 288 4050

Homeopathy: Society of Homeopaths, **www.homeopathy-soh.org**, 0845 450 6622

Hypnotherapy: Glenn Harrold, **www.glennharrold.com**

Noise pollution: Noise Resource Service, **www.noisere-source.org** 020 7329 0774

Nutritional Therapy: Sally Child, **www.nutritionfirst.co.uk**, 023 8027 5646

Sleep clinics: Papworth Hospital, **www.papworthpeople.com**, 01480 830541

The London Sleep Centre, **www.londonsleepcentre.com**

Sleep research: University of Loughborough Sleep Research Centre, **www.lboro.ac.uk/departments/hu/groups/sleep/**, 01509 223091

Snoring and Sleep Apnoea: British Snoring and Sleep Apnoea Association, **www.britishsnoring.co.uk**, 01737 245638

We've put together a list of useful organisations to contact if you have trouble sleeping. As contact details often change we've put the list on our website where we can keep it updated. You can find this at **www.whiteladderpress.com** – just click on 'Useful contacts' next to the information about this book.

If you don't have access to the Internet you can contact White Ladder by any of the means on the next page and we'll print off a hard copy and post it to you free of charge.